AWAKENING

THE HIGHER SELF

A JOURNEY INTO YOUR SOUL

TERRA SONORA

Published by:
The Center of Oneness
P.O. Box 531
Sedona, AZ 86339
(888) 485-0111
www.centerofoneness.com
www.angelchannel.com

Design and layout:
www.Budgetbookdesign.com

Printed by:
RJ Communications LLC
www.Booksjustbooks.com
International Standard Book Number (ISBN): 0-9744729-0-5

Printed in the United States of America

First printing: June 2000
Second printing: March 2001
Third Printing: March 2003
Fourth Printing: August 2003

My thanks to Kiki for her lovely artwork found on pages 17, 30, 95, 103 and 155

TABLE OF CONTENTS

"Be proud of yourselves, dear ones,
acknowledge the growth,
proclaim the power, and know
the beauty of all that you are.
Share with others the greatness
that is within you, so that all
may know the shining star
of your soul."

"ONE"

INTRODUCTION

I feel truly blessed and humbled by my abilities to communicate so easily with the angelic realm. I have come to know and love my guardian angels and spirit guides with all my heart and soul. They are trusted friends to me, and they fill me with love every day.

My spiritual journey in this life started in 1986 when a friend of mine at the time (oddly enough, named Angel) gave me a book about reincarnation that changed my life forever. It was "Past Lives, Future Loves" by Dick Sutphen[1]. It opened my mind to the concept that our soul or higher self is able to survive physical death and be reborn into another body, lifetime after lifetime. I then read the book "Messages from Michael" by Chelsea Quinn Yarbro[2] which further helped me to understand that there is a reason to this reincarnation cycle… to learn, to grow, to evolve and to return to God.

After that, I began to meditate, and pursued my spiritual growth with great enthusiasm. I read every new age or metaphysical book I could get my hands on. I started to think more about my life's purposes and the lessons I was meant to learn in this lifetime. I was determined to learn my lessons and move forward in my personal and spiritual evolution as fast as I possibly could. Be careful what you wish for! It threw me into years of looking at every issue, and every fear I ever had was right in my face. I immersed myself into my personal healing process. No one said a spiritual path was an easy one! Working with angels will certainly speed up your personal growth!

What kept me going was that I believed if I could integrate my life lessons, be free of fear and stay centered in God's love, then life would be easier, and more blessed. I was right, but I think it's an illusion to think you will never have an issue or challenge again. The difference is that we can learn how to process our issues and challenges more quickly and move into acceptance, understanding and integration without lingering too long in suffering. As we come to know our higher self we can find inner peace more easily and be comforted by our oneness with God.

In 1987 a dear friend of mine was training to become a certified hypnotherapist and was looking for someone to practice on, so I volunteered. He began the session by asking me to close my eyes and visualize myself on a beautiful ocean beach. By listening to his soothing voice and following his guidance, I relaxed and found myself slipping into an altered state of consciousness. While in that open and aware state, I spontaneously started channeling one of my spirit guides. It felt good, so I did not fight it. It was loving, and the words spoken through me were very assuring and insightful. My friend, who was very spiritual and familiar with channeling, continued the session by talking with my spirit guide.

After he brought me back to full consciousness, he said, "Wow! That was great! How long have you been channeling?" I could barely contain myself as I excitedly said, "That was my first time!"

Believe it or not, my mother had taken me to a channeler for a session the year before, so the concept of channeling was familiar to me. I realized that channeling was not difficult for me and I got very excited that I could do this. I began to practice channeling with my friends and family. Over the years my channeling kept getting better and better. The wisdom that was given to me by the angels helped me to be more aware of the "big picture" of life. I began to really understand my higher purposes and my reasons for being. I knew my life's purposes would be fulfilled by serving God and humanity.

Some days I feel like the luckiest person on the planet, because I am so sure of my life's purposes, and I know in my heart that I am fulfilling God's highest plan for me. When I channel the angels, they fill me with tremendous love, joy, and healing energy. It is always a beautiful experience for me.

I honor my relationship with the Christ Consciousness (Jesus in his ascended form) and the Mother Mary. To me, Christ and Mary represent embodiments of the God/Goddess essence in human form. When I connect with these powerful and miraculous beings they are filled with so much intense love and compassion for all of humanity, that it often brings tears to my eyes. Christ spoke to me and asked me to bring through messages of love and empowerment for humanity.

I have been so blessed to know their presence and to be graced by their love. I share this with you because the purity and integrity of my work is extremely important to me. I know that my spiritual beliefs may be different from many, but as an Interfaith Minister, I believe there are many pathways to God's love. We are all just seeking truth. Each person must follow their heart to find their own unique spiritual path.

I would like to introduce you to my own special group of angels and spirit guides. I primarily work with an entity named "ONE." They are wonderful beings of light from the celestial and angelic realms. They have said that if counted individually, they would be about 100 souls, however they have blended their energies as a single consciousness and speak as one. I feel privileged to have them in my life and I'm honored to share their love and wisdom with the world.

They conclude every channeling session by saying, "We are ONE." It is interesting that they are not only identifying themselves, but they are simultaneously expressing their core spiritual belief. They teach that we are all *one* with God/Goddess/All That Is/Creator/Source. The essence of the Divine is in each of our souls. If you become more aware of your higher self, you ascend your consciousness to the higher realms and can experience for yourself the bliss of the oneness of All That Is.

I consider myself to be a fairly normal and grounded person. I worked in the legal profession for 20 years, but gave it up in 1998 to pursue my spiritual work full time. I am blessed with many wonderful and loving relationships in my life. I can honestly say I have had a blessed life and I know that there are wonderful miracles and many joys ahead of me.

This book is a compilation of my spiritual understandings and transcriptions of channeled messages from ONE. In many chapters, ONE has added a guided meditation to help you personalize and integrate the wisdom they share. I've included information to help you learn how to meditate, how to channel, how to communicate with loved ones on the other side, and how to create more joy in your life.

To further support your journey into your soul, I have created a guided meditation CD also called "Awakening the Higher Self" to accompany this book. The three meditations on the CD are set to beautiful music, and will gently guide you through a relaxation process. The first meditation will help you to meet your angels and spirit guides, as outlined in Chapter 3. Another meditation will help you discover your true life's purposes, as described in Chapter 4. The third one is a quick 13-minute meditation, created to help you open to receive healing energy and Divine wisdom from the angels.

Ordering information can be found on the last page of this book, or visit my website at www.angelchannel.com.

I hope you can feel the truth in the channeled material in this book. I invite you to hear this information with an open heart, welcome in whatever feels right for you and let go of the rest. It is my hope that you become more aware of your higher self - the part of you that lives in perfect harmony with God's love.

Terra Sonora

CHAPTER 1

WHAT IS THE HIGHER SELF?

I believe that one of the most powerful steps on your spiritual path is to become aware that you are more than a physical body. I have come to know and recognize that I have a soul or a spirit within this body that is eternal. I call this part of me the higher self.

One of my core beliefs is that we are all children of God. I believe humanity is so dear to God because we are creations of the Creator. Just as we carry the DNA of our biological parents, I feel we carry an energy of the Creator within our soul. It makes sense to me that we carry the essence of the Divine within us.

Consider your higher self to be your "God Self" or eternal self. I believe our soul, our spirit, can live in the higher dimensions of the nonphysical realms. The higher self is the part of us that knows all, sees all, and is always at one with All That Is.

We have all had those moments when we are extraordinary beings. There are times that we say amazing things or we show remarkable courage and strength, and we have no idea where it came from. There are times we feel bigger than life, that maybe God is working through us. This is evidence that your higher self is alive and well.

To begin awakening your higher self, you must first acknowledge that it exists within you! Embrace the part of you that is Divine! Fortunately, we are not alone in this endeavor. As we begin to become more aware of our own spirit, we can simultaneously become more aware of other spirits as well! Namely, angels, spirit guides, ascended masters, saints, archangels, and other beings of light and aspects of

God/Goddess/All That Is.

The beings of light that dwell in the angelic realm are very attentive and filled with concern for our well-being. Our angels and spirit guides love us deeply, human foibles and all. They only want the best for us. They are emissaries of God to help us in our too often struggle for happiness.

Taking time for meditation is one of the greatest gifts of time you can give to yourself (it's right up there with a full body massage and energy healing session!). Meditation does not have to be a complicated process. It can be as simple as taking a few deep breaths, clearing the mind and opening your heart to God's love.

CHAPTER 2

CREATING SACRED SPACE FOR YOUR MEDITATIONS

If you are new to meditation, I have some suggestions for you to help you get started. I offer you some practical information to help you create sacred space for your spiritual work and make the most of your meditation time.

Approach your meditation time as sacred time for your spiritual practice. Give yourself the chance to develop a wonderful relationship with your angels and spirit guides. I know they have many gifts of love to offer you.

Set aside some quiet time and go to a peaceful part of your home, where you can have some privacy. Create a sacred space in your home by setting aside even one corner of one room to be your meditation space. Have a comfortable chair there, with a small place to set a glass of water and perhaps create a small altar.

On your altar you can place sacred objects that represent your own unique spirituality. For some of you, that might be a picture of Christ, Mother Mary, Buddha, the Dali Lama, angels, or any other symbols that represent your personal spiritual beliefs. You can add pictures of loved ones to pray for, or a prayer list, and maybe some crystals to help amplify the positive energies you bring in. You may also want to light a candle, burn some incense, or scent the air with pure essential oils. You can also "smudge" yourself, by lighting a traditional Native American smudge stick (made of sage and cedar) and fanning the smoke through your aura. Smudging is a wonderful way to purify and cleanse your energies. Burning incense or smudging can also help you hold a focused state. The key is to create a special, sacred place that honors your spiritual intentions.

You may also find it helpful to play soft, relaxing, new age music in the background. I've included in the back of this book a list of some of my favorite meditation music. Also, holding a crystal while you meditate can amplify positive energies. A wonderful resource for crystals and crystal singing bowls is also included in the back of the book in the Resource section.

When you set aside your meditation time, close the door, turn the phone off and settle in for some quiet relaxation. You can sit or lie down, but if you are tired, lying down will likely put you to sleep. Take a nap if you need it, but if you are planning to meditate, sitting up may help you to remain fully aware of your meditation experience.

Keep a very simple approach to meditation. It is simply quieting the mind and allowing your inner self or higher self to be fully present. Take some deep cleansing breaths to release all tension from your body. Take a moment to move your neck and shoulders around to release the stress and tension that many of us hold in that part of our body. Then settle in and completely relax.

I always work with white light and love from the heart of God, which, to me is the center core of Creator/Source. Whatever your spiritual orientation, try to acknowledge some form of a higher power or a Creator Source of Energy in the Universe. At a deep spiritual level, we resonate with the pure, loving essence of God. As you open to the awareness of your own pure loving soul essence, you truly awaken your higher self.

I invite you to consider what the energy of God would feel like to you. Open to that energy in whatever form that feels right for you. In my meditations I always begin by visualizing white light pouring into me from the heart of God/Goddess/All That Is. I set forth my intention to open my heart to receive pure loving energy from the Creator Source.

Then I begin to feel my energy or aura expand and I sense my higher self within me.

During your meditation you can direct that Divine energy to raise your own vibration, to be more in harmony with God's highest light. I invite you to take some time to just be with this energy and take God's light and love into your own heart.

I find it helpful to use visualizations to move beyond our third dimensional perspectives. For example, visualizing a beautiful place in nature like a tropical waterfall, can sometimes get us out of thinking with our busy-brain and induce relaxation. Don't worry if you think that you are not visualizing clearly enough. It sometimes takes practice to develop your third-eye sight. The intention here is to simply enjoy this process in a gentle way, without self-judgment. If you have difficulty "seeing" things in your mind's eye, start out by pretending to see the visualizations, using your imagination, until your intuitive vision becomes more clear.

Visualizations in your meditations can be used to reach a higher state of consciousness. Unleash your creativity and allow your playful imagination the freedom to create beautiful environments for your higher self. Have fun with this and keep your intentions centered in love.

Everyone has the ability to perceive spirit realms with their intuitive, visual, auditory or kinesthetic senses. You may find that you are stronger in one or more of these areas. When you are in meditation and you ask to experience the energy of your spirit guides and angels, be open to seeing, hearing and feeling their presence. Over time you will come to recognize each guide or angel by their own unique energy signature. They may appear surrounded in a particular color, you may "hear" them in a certain tone of voice, or they may come in with a particular feeling of love or warmth.

Keep in mind that the messages you receive in meditation may continue to unfold over the next few days and/or weeks. Once you set forth your intention to receive from the Universe, keep an open heart and an open mind as to how those intentions are manifested in your life. Spirit will continue to work with you, even after you have completed your meditation.

In this work, as in all spiritual work, be discerning. Set forth your intention to work with the highest and most loving angels and spirit guides. If you encounter an energy that is uncomfortable or perceived to be negative in any way, command it to leave in the name of God. Surround yourself with more white light and call upon God's highest angels, seraphim, and Ascended Masters of Light to be with you. Allow the light of God to protect you and you will know that you are safe.

I encourage you to practice meditation to deepen your awareness of your higher self. I have outlined below a very simple meditation process to help you get started. There are many suggested meditations in this book and I feel it would be easiest for you to start each of them with this simple four-step process.

FOUR-STEP PROCESS TO BEGIN YOUR MEDITATIONS

1. **GET COMFORTABLE.** Settle into your sacred space, or any quiet place, and close your eyes. Stretch a little, moving your neck and shoulders around to release any tension you might be holding in your body. Then allow your body to completely relax.

2. **BREATHE.** Take some deep breaths to relax the body even more. Tell your busy brain that its only job right now is to focus on breathing and think about the feeling of the oxygen and energy flowing through your body.

3. **INVITE GOD.** Invite God/Goddess/All That Is to join with you. Imagine that there is a large column of white light from Creator/Source coming all the way down through your body from the top of your head to your toes, filling your body with light and Divine healing energy.

4. **SURRENDER.** Release the need to control your meditation and go with the flow of energy. Feel your light body or higher self come alive. Allow yourself to feel lighter, and free from the physical realm. Open to the higher dimensions centered in God's love and BE your higher self.

CHAPTER 3

CHANNELING ANGELS AND SPIRIT GUIDES

The Angelic Realm is filled with infinite gifts of love from the heart of God/Goddess. Our guardian angels and spirit guides can offer us loving, healing energy as well as valuable insight from their unique perspective. Accessing these higher dimensions and feeling connected to our angels can strengthen our souls and help us enjoy the flow of life.

WHAT IS CHANNELING?

Simply put, channeling is the ability to quiet the busy mind, attune to the higher vibrational frequencies of the angelic and celestial realms, and bring through messages of love and wisdom from spirit guides and angels. Sometimes the messages may be from the higher self or God self, which can also be of a pure and truthful nature.

There is a level of integrity that must be maintained in this work so as to not allow your personal thoughts and feelings to interfere with the information coming from spirit. There is a place of centered truth within all of us and channeling, in its pure form, will always resonate with that place of truth inside you.

To maintain the highest level of integrity in this work, be sure you only work with the highest and most loving spirit guides, angels, Archangels, Ascended Masters, etc., who resonate with the vibrational frequency of the love and light of God. Bring in God's white light or ask Christ (or other God-embodiment) to keep the energy of love and protection around you. There is nothing to fear when you invoke God's light and love.

Know as well that you are worthy enough to be calling on the Christ. Do not ever feel that you would be "bothering Him" for any small thing. The Christ that I know loves each and every one of us. He is there for you in every way. Call upon Him for protection, support, friendship, guidance and love. Likewise, the Mother Mary and beings like St. Germain, St. Francis, the Archangels, the Ascended Masters, Buddha, Sai Baba, Krishna, the Dali Lama, etc. are all available to us for love, protection and support.

PREPARING TO CHANNEL

I always found that practicing channeling with others was easier for me than practicing alone. However, taking time for solitude and meditation was also important to help strengthen my connection with my higher self, angels and spirit guides. Whether alone or with someone, take some time to sit quietly. Create a sacred space and prepare for meditation as described in my "Four-Step Meditation Process" at the end of Chapter 2. I usually light a candle (I prefer white or pink) and I love to burn nag champa incense from India to create a sacred environment. Sometimes I will play my crystal singing bowl or Tibetan brass singing bowl to raise my vibration even higher. Always visualize and feel the white light from the heart of God/Goddess/All That Is flowing into you.

It can be powerful to start with a prayer or invocation. Some recite the Lord's Prayer, or create a simple prayer blessing of their own. I really love "The Great Invocation" originally channeled by Alice A. Bailey[3] . I know there are many people devoted to Alice Bailey's teachings, which are profoundly beautiful. I was guided to modify The Great Invocation for my personal spiritual practice. I offer my revised version here in love:

"THE GREAT INVOCATION"
(Originally by Alice A. Bailey, As Modified by Terra Sonora)

Straight from the Heart of God
Love pours forth into my soul;
May all know that God dwells within.

Straight from the Light of God
Peace and tranquility clear my mind.
May God's Light awaken each soul.

Straight from the Wisdom of God
I am guided to fulfill my life purposes.
May each one honor their Divine gifts.

Straight from the Kingdom of God,
comes unity and oneness with all.
May the souls of humanity know love.

Straight from the Intention of God,
many helpers come into my life.
May we all receive with joy.

Straight from my own heart
The love of God shines forth.
May all know the God that I AM.

When I work in groups I often use a healing and cleansing prayer to raise everyone's vibration and set the tone. I have combined some suggested prayers from the teachings of Dr. Joshua David Stone [4] and added some of my own to it. Here is the prayer I use:

Cleansing and Healing Prayer

Collectively we call in the energies of God/Goddess/ All-That-Is to join with us and manifest in our hearts as pure Divine, Loving, Healing Energy.

We call in the Energies of Christ, Mother Mary, the Archangels, the Seraphim, the Ascended Masters and all our Spirit Guides and Angels to join with us and hold the light of sacred space around us.

We call forth the violet flame of Saint Germain to bathe our entire being in his powerful violet transmuting flame. Let this beautiful violet energy, flowing from the Heart of God, transmute any and all negativity into the purity and love of God.

We call forth the Golden Light of the Christ Consciousness and allow it to bathe our entire being in the energy of love.

We call forth our own Healing Angels to energize and heal all our chakras.

We open to the beauty of our own spirit. So be it.

The Invocation and Prayer can help you create a higher vibrational environment for this work. When you have taken a few moments to breathe deeply, while visualizing the white light, you will stay centered and connected to that still, peaceful place inside your heart.

HOW TO CONNECT
WITH YOUR ANGELS AND GUIDES

I believe everyone has an angel that is always with you, and who loves you very much. It is good to start your channeling practice with that angel. Everyone also has at least one spirit guide, or perhaps several, and if you feel a stronger pull to work with a specific spirit guide, then do that. Telepathically call out to your angels and spirit guides to come and be with you in your sacred space. In your mind's eye begin to see them coming to you. When you feel their presence, imagine that a beam of light begins to radiate from your angel's or guide's heart to yours. Open your heart and begin to feel their love for you. Feel the energy flowing both ways from their heart to yours and your heart to theirs. Once that energy is flowing strongly, imagine a second beam of light radiating from their third eye to yours. Feel the flow of energy between your third eye and theirs and allow all your senses (and your chakras) to awaken.

I have found that connecting both the heart and the third eye strengthens the telepathic communication link. If you are comfortable, invite your angel to come and blend with you. There is nothing to fear here. If you feel and discern that your angel radiates a God-centered loving energy, there is absolutely no harm can come to you in allowing your angel to come close to you. There are no ulterior motives in the angelic realm, they simply want to love you and help you. I let my angels come right into me and blend with me. It's as if we share the same space for a while and since they are pure Divine light, it's not the least bit crowded!

Once in that state, open to the bliss of the oneness. The angels and guides of the highest light always come in with tremendous loving energy. It should feel comforting, soothing and uplifting.

If you feel any fear and uncomfortableness, focus on bringing in more white light. Ask yourself, "What am I afraid of?" Try to let go of your fears and understand that you have complete control over what you allow into your energy field. Proclaim your power!

WORKING WITH GOD

If you have any doubts about what you are connecting with, or are not too sure yet about angels and spirit guides, just work directly with God. I believe that God is so vast that it may be difficult for some to comprehend a form of God that they can relate to. I would suggest you pick any God-embodiment that you can identify as being pure, Divine loving energy. I usually see God/Goddess/All That Is as a brilliant central sun, like thousands of suns, but pulsating with energy, with love and with immense intelligence. I see Christ as being one of the primary human embodiments of God. Christ, as the Master Jesus, was able to embody the essence, love and purity of God in perhaps the most perfected state a human was capable of achieving at the time. He was a role model for all of us, and he taught us how to embody the essence of God into our lives. If that resonates with you, work with Christ. If there is another aspect of God that resonates more strongly with you, work with that being of light.

WORKING WITH ANGELS AND SPIRIT GUIDES

To strengthen your connection with your angels and guides, you can simply acknowledge their presence in your life. Talk to them telepathically, and trust that they hear you. They respond to you and it just takes an open-ness on your part to "hear" them. They may communicate by a vision, words or a feeling of knowingness.

While you are in meditation, ask your angels or spirit guides to identify themselves by name. Be in an open, receptive state and you will likely perceive their names in response. If a name feels right, use it to converse with your angel or guide to help strengthen your relationship with them. If you do not hear a particular name, focus on their energy signature and try to feel a name that resonates with their vibration. Then select a name that you feel fits, and start calling them that. The angels or guides will honor that name or otherwise let you know if they prefer a different name. Think about it. If someone starts calling you by a name that is not your name, you would certainly let that person know if you did not like it. On the other hand, if it felt like a term of endearment, you just might like it when they call you that. That is how the angels feel about it too. I can just hear them now, "Oh how sweet - she wants to call me Lilly!" They love that!

Keep a journal or notebook and pen or tape recorder handy when you meditate. You just may receive a profound message that you will feel compelled to record in some way. This allows you to work with the message until it feels integrated. It also allows you the opportunity to share the message with others, to validate your experience.

If there is any aspect of your life that you would like clarity or insight about, go into mediation and ask your angels and guides to help you. Pray with them and God to help manifest the healing or joyful circumstances you seek. Create an open feeling within you to receive their blessings and guidance. Trust that you will be able to discern what is truth for you. Your true guides and angels will never lead you astray, and will always guide you along the path of your highest and greatest destiny.

By practicing the exercises above, you can come to know your guides and angels in a deep and profound way. In these chaotic and busy times, taking a moment to connect with your spirit guides and angels can give you the reassurance you need. Even if you don't have a specific question, connect with your healing angels to send you healing energy to balance and energize you.

VERBAL CHANNELING SKILLS

It is wonderful to work with your angels and guides in meditation. If you are able to bring through loving messages for others, that is a form of channeling. Some people write down messages, like taking dictation from the angel or spirit guide, which is called automatic writing. That is another form of channeling.

Personally, I feel the most powerful form of channeling is when an angel, spirit guide or entity comes fully into the body of the channeler and speaks directly to others. This is the form of channeling that I practice most often. I have developed such a strong relationship with ONE, that I can easily feel their energy. After bringing in white light, I invite them to blend with me. It is not long before I hear their loving words, "Fear not, dear one, we are with you." There are certain physiological responses I experience in the process, such as the left side of my face twitches and scrunches up a bit. I feel them come into me and its like an expansion. Suddenly my aura feels like it is ten feet across. A strong but peaceful, loving feeling comes over me.

The issue of trust is important here. I would not surrender my body to any entity, that's for sure. Ask the angel or being to prove to you that it is of the light. Again, if there is any uncomfortableness, command it to leave. However, if it feels loving and angelic in energy, and your gut tells you it is safe and pure, you can allow the energy to blend with you.

The moment of surrender may be different for each person. For me, it is an allowing of ONE to come and be fully present. Sometimes I visualize my favorite sacred tree in Sedona, Arizona to help me let go. This is the part that takes practice. It is not for everyone, but if you are guided to practice channeling in this way, partner up with a loving friend whom you trust with all your heart, and have fun with it. Your partner can ask your angel or guide a question or simply ask if they have a message for them. Do not try to think of the answer, just let it flow through you and say what you feel your angel or spirit guide wants you to say.

Do not be alarmed if the tone or pitch of your voice changes slightly when a being is speaking through you. They have their own energy signature that may be different from yours and they will utilize your voice in the way that best expresses who they are.

My own guides speak through me with a Celtic or Irish accent. In the beginning I felt embarrassed that my voice changed, so I would try to stay present, channel in my normal tone of voice, and just relay messages. With that approach, I felt like I was too much in the way, so I had to let go of feeling embarrassed and just surrender more to the process. That is when my channeling abilities really took off. I let go of the need to control the process and just allowed them to speak through me.

Be sure you really open your heart and let in their love for you. This can be quite profound and can help you to understand how the angels perceive you.

CHANNELING VS. MEDIUMSHIP

Channeling is not necessarily the same thing as mediumship. While there are some channelers who can act as mediums, and some mediums are excellent channelers, I'd like to try to explain the difference. As I have come to understand, a medium is focused on primarily bringing through messages from deceased loved ones. A channeler is focused on primarily bringing through messages from angels and spirit guides. The lines of distinction become even thinner when a deceased loved one happens to be dwelling in the angelic realms and is acting like a spirit guide to their loved ones left behind.

When I channel for my clients, it is not unusual for someone to ask if there is a message from a particular deceased loved. We (ONE and I) ask for the deceased person's full name. We then send out a telepathic call to that soul and wait a few seconds for them to show themselves to us. Most of the time they come when called. I find it interesting that sometimes the loved ones have specific messages that offer validating details of their life, and other times, the messages are simply that they are at peace and they send their love. Since we have no control over what the deceased loved ones will want to tell us, it can be difficult if a client has certain expectations that the spirits must provide hard core proof of their existence. Sometimes spirit simply will not play that game.

While I have facilitated countless profound healing experiences between deceased loved ones and their survivors, it is always my preference to keep my focus on channeling the energies of the angelic realm. Mediumship can sometimes be emotionally draining and I honor the brave souls who have taken on that particular task of serving humanity. Over the years I've learned some techniques to minimize the stress of mediumship work, but I am not immune to feeling the deep sense of loss that tragic deaths can bring. My heart is full of compassion for those who have lost loved ones.

The channeling work that I do is rarely draining upon me. I have had channeling days of back-to-back appointments from 10 a.m. to 10 p.m. (with breaks, of course) and would actually feel energized at the end of the day. I have always felt that if someone feels completely drained after giving a channeling session, then they may be putting too much of themselves into it or somehow resisting the energies. I believe that if you open up to the Divine loving energy of the Creator, you can be filled with tremendous energy so that the spirit works through you, and not draining your own energies in the process. Any tiredness from a long day like that would be just from the effort of holding a focus for that long. For me, keeping the channeling link strong is about holding the focus, holding the energy of the spirit and staying in that altered state for the entire duration of the session.

If you plan to do more than an hour or two of channeling,

drink plenty of water to prevent dehydration. The high vibrational energy running through your body may slightly elevate your body temperature. Drinking vitamin-enriched water, sports water or protein drinks will help you maintain balanced blood sugar levels and keep your energy high. After a long day of channeling I usually feel a little light-headed, so I take some deep breaths, drink more water, eat some food, listen to rock and roll music, or walk in the fresh air to feel grounded in my body again.

TRANCE CHANNELING VS. CONSCIOUS CHANNELING

There are some channelers who fall into a deep trance, similar to sleep. They channel messages from spirit and when they are done, they "wake up" and often do not remember anything that was said. Personally, I always wanted to hear what was being said and benefit from the loving advice they gave to others, so I trained myself to stay aware during the entire process.

There are some very good psychics and mediums who are actually conscious channelers. They remain fully conscious, with eyes open, and are actually connecting with their higher self, angels and spirit guides during their readings. They pull the information psychically, from the higher realms, and when connected in this way, the information will be respectful of your free will, true and supportive. The best conscious channelers can communicate messages from the higher realms while staying fully present in their body. That is truly an art!

I use and teach a middle-of-the-road approach. I prefer to go into a light trance or meditative state. I stay conscious of what is going on in the room, but my energies are enough out of the way that I feel the pure messages of spirit and the loving energy of the angels coming through with clarity. It is an altered state of consciousness where you remain fully awake and aware. By practicing meditation, and the techniques offered here, you can create that altered state at will.

REVERENCE AND RESPECT

I hope this has helped to explain channeling in more detail for those who are interested in this area of spiritual exploration. Channeling can be safe, when treated with respect. Understand that you are slightly vulnerable in that altered state (believe me, you don't want your big dog running into the room and jumping on you when you are channeling!) You can equate it to a deep peaceful sleep. No one likes the feeling of your spirit being "slammed" back into your body when jarred abruptly. And you do not want to invite "any spirit" to just jump in. Be very specific in what types of beings (i.e. loving and God-like) that you attract and work with.

Honor the sacredness of your communications with spirit. Approach it with reverence and profound respect. Open your heart to receive the many gifts of spirit and you will be overwhelmed with gratitude for the abundance of love and blessings in your life. I wish you much joy and love in your explorations with angels and spirit guides.

CHAPTER 4

MEDITATING ON YOUR LIFE'S PURPOSE

Have you ever asked yourself "Why am I here?" and wondered about your life's purpose? Is your life predestined in some way or is it all choice? The answer is likely yes to both. Perhaps you came into this lifetime with specific purposes to fulfill but you have free will choice to do them or not.

Perhaps you are blessed, as I feel I am, to know with certainty that you are here to serve humanity in some way. If that seems like your life's purpose, you have the delightful task of figuring out how. The joy of this adventure can be the freedom of free will choice, but sometimes we can feel overwhelmed at all our infinite options. Or perhaps you are stuck in neutral and don't know what to do next.

Let's suppose you would like to fulfill your highest and greatest destiny here on earth. What would that look like to you? How does that feel? Can you hear your inner voice gently guiding you? Why not take a meditative journey to find these answers from within.

Everyone has spirit guides and angels that are always there for you. One of their many purposes is to help you stay on course in your life's journey. They are always willing to offer their gentle guidance and to help you along your path. To hear their messages more clearly, open your heart to the immense love they feel for you, and the channels will open.

In one of my meditation groups ONE came through with a beautiful meditation on the subject of finding your life's purpose. The meditation included a guided visual journey to a crystal castle in a mystical realm, like a grand library of the universe. At this place each of us found one special crystal that was programmed with our life's purpose. We spent time with this crystal and with our spirit guides to journey deep into our soul to receive answers to questions like "Who am I? and "Why am I here?". The meditation was so insightful and enjoyable, I wanted to share it with you in this Chapter.

In this channeled meditation, the "soul crystal" is a good tool for unlocking the secrets of your soul. Think of it as a useful metaphor to access your own higher self.

If you are seeking some clarity about your life's purposes, please take some time for yourself to meditate. Consider your spiritual growth and personal development a priority in your life now. Charting your course now will make for smoother sailing later on. Set aside some "alone time" to sit in a quiet place. You may wish to find a beautiful place in nature or meditate in your own sacred space. Holding a crystal during this particular meditation is especially helpful.

You may wish to read through this meditation now and set aside the time to guide yourself through it or you may wish to tape record yourself reading this meditation slowly, and then play it back for yourself so that you can enjoy the meditative journey in a more relaxed state. If you do tape yourself, give plenty of pause time in between the questions asked to give yourself the time you'll need. Or if you prefer, you can listen to this meditation on my CD "Awakening the Higher Self" (information is on the last page of this book).

MEDITATION TO DISCOVER YOUR LIFE'S PURPOSES

To begin your meditation, use my "Four-Step Meditation Process" outlined at the end of Chapter 2.

Imagine the Heart of God descending upon you, giving you a loving and peaceful feeling. Also welcome the Christ Consciousness, the Mother Mary Energies, the Archangels, and your own Angels and Master Teacher Spirit Guides to join with you, asking them to amplify the energies of light.

Open yourself to becoming the light. With each breath you become more relaxed and at peace, aware of the light within you.

Begin to open your mind and open your spirit to the higher dimensions, and begin to feel your light body ascending, as we are going on a journey, a magical journey to the fifth dimension. Today you are seeking a very special place: There is an immense crystal castle that is a sacred temple, with a crystal Hall of Records. Imagine this great library of the universe. See the beauty of this magical place with huge crystal columns, twinklings of rainbows everywhere, and rays of sunlight dancing through this crystal palace. It is a warm and inviting place, and it is a place that your soul has been before. There is something familiar about it.

In this great hall of crystal records, there is a place that is just for you. Imagine yourself traveling through this incredible place, as you are guided to a very special crystal, a crystal that has been programmed by your soul. Find your special crystal, as it contains all the wisdom of all your lifetimes, past, present, future. Find yourself with this crystal now, as it radiates the essence of your soul. And as your guides and angels join with you in this magical place, it is time for you to touch and to be with this crystal, and receive its messages that you need now to help you on your path. Hold your magical crystal and receive your messages now.

In this crystal there may be a message about what you are completing or perhaps a final block that you must move through. Ask this crystal "What is it of the past that is complete now?"

In this magical crystal that is you, ask to see the light, to see the deep truth that you know within your soul.

Ask this crystal, as you hold it close to you, to reveal to you your life's purposes here.

And there is even more in your life's purpose, look deeper and see it, know it, and feel it.

Inside this crystal, deep within your soul's programming, is your highest and greatest destiny, the most positive future, your greatest future. Allow the crystal to show you what is possible.

Inside this crystal is the "big picture", the view of everyone, all the supportive people in your life, friends, family, guides and angels, all helping you along the way. See, inside the crystal, how the universe will provide everything you need to support you on your life's path.

And now this crystal becomes an instrument of light, as the powerful Creator/Source ushers in a beam of pure divine energy to illuminate this crystal and to supercharge it with the energy of God/Goddess. Feel the energy of this crystal amplifying your greatest destiny, supercharging your dreams. Feel this crystal come alive with an intense energy of manifestation.

At this time put into the crystal your own hopes, dreams and wishes for this lifetime. Program now your free will choices into your soul crystal.

Feel the energy of the crystal amplify as it feeds your dreams and wishes. Your guides and angels surround you, programming the crystal with their love and blessings. Feel the love and support from your guides and angels.

And lastly, there is one more secret this crystal holds for you. Open to receive that magical secret now.

The energies and the messages that you have received from your crystal are complete for now and it is time to place the crystal back within the crystal Hall of Records, in its rightful place, as a member of this magical place. Know that you can return to this magical crystal castle at any time to work with your crystal in consciously programming your highest and greatest destinies.

And so it is time to bid a fond "farewell for now" as you gently collect yourself, and slowly find your way back, to your third dimensional reality. Come back to this time and place, knowing that all the messages, visions and gifts are yours to keep, remembering the light of who you are. Give thanks to your higher self and honor all that you are. When you are ready, return to full consciousness, feeling balanced and energized.

I hope you have enjoyed the meditation, but before I close, my loving spirit guides "ONE" would like to share a message with you.

MESSAGE FROM ONE ON YOUR HIGHER PURPOSES

ONE: "When we speak of your highest and greatest destinies and your greatest dreams, we want you to know that those are very personal to you. Do not feel that you must accomplish anything at all. Your true life's purpose is within your inner heart and your inner knowingness. It may be that you are just meant to be the radiant human being that you are, and perhaps by being yourself you will inspire others to find the God/Goddess within themselves. Perhaps your greatest destiny is to be the greatest listener, the greatest giver, or perhaps it is to be the light-bearer and the truth-bearer. We know that you may have specific goals and dreams, and we encourage that, but do not underestimate the importance of your day-to-day being-ness, because truly you radiate the light of who you are, and truly you touch the hearts of others simply by being open and honoring the love that is within you at all times.

Know as well, dear ones, that indeed there is much in the way of guidance available to you. We know it seems that your choices may appear to be overwhelming and unlimited upon your physical plane. It may be that there are many, many options and so it might be difficult to know which way to turn. Know that you can trust your intuition when it comes from your heart. Even then, you may still hear that little voice of doubt in your mind that is questioning you. To get clear answers, take a few moments to enter a quiet meditation. Ask your gut, your soul, and call in your spirit guides and angels to come and be with you. They can reinforce a positive feeling or reinforce a "maybe not" feeling when you are weighing your decisions and choices. And believe us when we tell you that your guides and angels will help bring through an energy of "YES! YES! YES!" when you are moving forward in the direction towards your highest and greatest purposes here.

Know as well you also have the joy of being human and that is a great privilege because you have the choice of saying 'to heck with it all, I'm going to plop myself on the sofa and enjoy myself in the front of the talking box for a while'. So understand that you have a choice in every moment to simply relax, be, and enjoy yourself, or to push forward. We encourage you to find that balance for yourself. Find balance in your life as much as you can with your giving and receiving. It is important. Give freely, but be sure to open your heart to receiving the love in return that is always there for you. Know, dear ones, that we love you so very much and indeed we extend our loving, healing energy to each and every one of you.

Know there is infinite love and energy available to all of you at all times. We encourage you, that in your day-to-day life, take a moment to simply open your heart, open all the chakras and say 'Yes, let me soak in it for awhile. Let me feel that love from the heart of God.'

We wish we could take you by the hand everyday and just hold your hand and tell you how much you are loved, how special you are, how grand your purposes are, how immense your capacity for joy is, and how immense your capacity to give and receive love. We want all of you to know that you are magical beings, that you are precious and special. You are the brave ones to have come here lifetime after lifetime, living this human experience over and over and over again. And sometimes your soul says, 'WHY? Aren't I done yet? Enough of this already!' And yet you come back, and for many of you, you come back to serve to give a hand to your fellow humanity to say, 'Come on. There is a light at the end of the tunnel. Life is not always a struggle. Choose the easy path.' And so dear ones, many of you are the teachers, the healers and the evolvers of humanity. There is no small life purpose here. Know your purposes, dear ones, know your gifts, follow your heart and honor the Creator that you are."

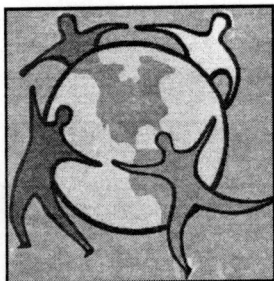

Chapter 5

Release your Past and Embrace the New You

ONE: "Greetings, dear ones. Indeed, this is a very exciting time for all of you to be alive! This is a time of magic, wonder, change and transformation. This is a time that truly the old patterns, the old ways of being of the past, are coming into the forefront of your consciousness, perhaps mirrored in another person, to help bring up the issues in your life that need to be released. Be aware that for some of you, your own deepest insecurities may come up to the surface. These are the very tough questions that may be uncomfortable to be asking yourself. Certainly, some of you are experiencing very difficult times, but we assure you, it is all for intense personal growth and transformation. This is a time in which much acceleration can occur in your own personal evolvement.

We want you to know dear ones, that if you have been able to experience the wonderful energies of this time and have been able to keep your spirits high with positive outlooks on your reality, then indeed you are adjusting to the higher energies very, very well. If perhaps you are seeing some chaos or disruption in the lives of others, it may be that perhaps you are meant to be the one to give some clarity of vision and clarity of insight to help them with their transformation process.

HONOR YOUR DIVINITY

Honor your Divine gifts and know your purposes here. Many of you are the healers, teachers, wisdom keepers, light bearers, and truth bringers, and are here to give positive support to your fellow humankind. This is a time that your soul, the

God-self deep within you, is wanting to come forth and be heard. This is a time, dear ones, of exploring your own intuitive powers, your abilities to connect with your own higher self and with the higher realms. Whether you choose to work with your spirit guides, angels, master teachers, ascended masters, or whatever God embodiment that feels wonderful and loving to you, this is the time to establish, deepen and strengthen those connections.

Dear ones, know that truly life is changing for everyone. We see the energies on this planet being enhanced, always increasing in vibrational frequency, helping each and every one of you to come to know the fullness of all that you are with more and more certainty, confidence and self love.

RELEASING THE PAST WITH EASE

We would like to talk to you about the subject of releasing. Yes, releasing and letting go of the past with love and with ease. Dear ones, know that the past has served you well. Love your past for the good that it created in your life. For even in the hard times, even in the pain, the struggle and the suffering, there have been gifts of spirit and gifts of strength that you have received, that have made you into the conscious, loving, compassionate being of light that sits within your body right now.

RELEASING NEGATIVITY

We want you to know dear ones, that as you choose it, life can be easier. You can release the negativity as it comes your way. We encourage you that as you come in contact with negative people, send them on their way, bless them, love them if you like, but let them go because you do not need to subject yourself to unnecessary negativity. Truly, dear ones, it is becoming more and more important that you honor that inner voice, that gut intuition, that is telling you to take good care of yourself. That same inner voice will tell you to surround yourself with positive loving people, who support you. For those people that are in your life, that are perhaps not as supportive, allow yourself a little bit of emotional distance. You need not waste your energy getting caught up in other people's dramas. It is alright to take good care of yourself. That is not being selfish in the negative sense of the word.

This is a time that can be emotional for some of you, and perhaps a bit perplexing as well. It can be a time of trying to decide what it is that you need to let go of. Examine yourself, examine your beliefs, your strengths, your wisdom and courage. Dear ones, know that each one of you will have those inner voices, your gut level, your higher self, your own God-self, if you will, come forth and talk to you and tell you of the life that lies ahead for you: the highest, most beautiful, most wonderful life that you can create for yourself. Your own highest and greatest destiny is always there, ever unfolding before you as you consciously choose it in your day-to-day life. Dear ones, as you allow your clear voice of truth to come forth from within you, you will be guided to your most magnificent destinies in this lifetime.

FORGIVENESS

This is a time to look within your heart and ask yourself if there anyone that you need to forgive. If the answer is yes, then know that this is the time to work on that. Bring the energy of love and compassion into your heart. If it is difficult to hold that energy while you think of the person who hurt you, welcome in the energies of the Christ or the Mother Mary to fill your heart with their love and compassion. Then let go of the pain, love them, forgive them, bless them, send them into the light and be free of it. Understand that you are meant to be light, free of negativity, and free of earthly burdens upon your spirit.

We encourage you dear ones, to always keep your channels open to receive infinite love and healing energy from the divine Creator Source to help replenish your energies. There is

Terra Sonora

no need to allow yourself to be drained by anyone. Understand that allowing others to drain you of your energy is an old pattern of your past that you do not have to bring into your present or future. As you allow yourself to always replenish your energies from the Creator Source, you cannot be drained by another. See this as a matter of choice.

Know as well dear ones, that you must understand that you are powerful beings of light. You have infinite strength, infinite wisdom, infinite abilities and there are those in your lives who may not know the appropriate way to respond to you at times. Be compassionate with them and understand they may be expecting you to be the 'old you' they have always known. Dear ones, while that 'old you' is still a part of you, there is so much more to who you are today.

PROCESSING FEAR

We want you to look within your soul and see if there is anything that you still fear. This can be difficult for some, because some fears have been suppressed in the subconscious for many years. The energy of fear is very much an old energy that belongs to the 1900's; it does not belong to the energies of 2000 and beyond. You live in a time where fear no longer serves a purpose. It is an old and outdated way of dealing with reality.

Whether it is an old fear of not being good enough, fear of failure or fear of death, do not be afraid of it dear ones. Embrace fear as one of your greatest teachers. Perhaps it has been an ally in the past, but it is like that old pair of jeans that doesn't quite zip up any more. You see, they just don't fit. We want you to know its alright to let go of them. If you need to, fold them up nicely and put them in a drawer somewhere so you can take them out and try them on again later, if you like. Most of all, we want you to know dear ones, that its alright to let them go, because fear has been replaced.

There is a shift in the greater consciousness of humankind that instead of feeling fear, there is understanding, awareness and respect. There is understanding of what is real and practical in your life and there is awareness of consequences. You can have a healthy respect for those things that could potentially cause your harm as they continue to exist in your realm. However, to fear those elements is to give away some of your power, to surrender a little bit of yourself.

Dear ones, we want you to know that you are as safe as you choose to acknowledge yourself to be. We want you to feel the power of your proclaiming your safety and knowing with certainty that, as you invoke the powers of God/Goddess/All That Is, and acknowledge your protection, it is so, without question. We want you to come to that level of confidence of knowingness that you are safe whenever you proclaim it to be your reality.

When you indulge yourself in fears like, what are other people thinking of me, or a nebulous fear of some big bad, awful thing that just might happen out there in the future somewhere, begin to see this as a form of self-abuse. Those are the type of fears that just have no purpose any longer. We want you to have the awareness that when a fear energy comes up, you can recognize it for what it is. If you need to, take a moment to go within, and ask yourself where does this fear have its origin. Is it one of those seeds planted in my childhood or adolescence? That level of introspection may not be necessary for you, but recognize the fear, let it go and find something to replace it with, such as a feeling of understanding, awareness or respect. You can use a positive affirmation, a positive statement of what is (as opposed to what you fear it could be), and honor your truth.

We want you to know that the more you can let go of fear and release the past, recognize that which no longer works in your life, and lovingly let it go, the more positive change will come into your life, like a breath of fresh air, dear ones.

FEAR OF CHANGE

There is no need to fear change. We know that that is at the heart of fears for many. We want you to know dear ones, that if you can embrace change, truly you embrace the fullness of the opportunities that are presented to you. It is good for you to survey you options, look around at all the infinite possibilities and allow yourself to be drawn to that which feels the best. So if you are compelled to make some changes in your life, trust that you are guided to make these changes for your own highest and greatest good and that letting go of the fears and negativities of the past, is not all that hard.

EMBRACING THE NEW YOU

We want explain our view of this "New You." It is about all of you, each one of our sacred, blessed humanities walking this earth, finding your higher selves, finding your higher purposes, finding your true divine gifts that are within you, and moving forward in your life with grace and ease and embracing all that you are. That dear ones, is the New Age. This is the time of enlightenment that so many have spoken of.

We want you to look ahead into your own many possible futures, and know that infinite doors of opportunities can open up to you as time progresses. We want you to know that you can create as many opportunities for yourself as you desire. Imagine your future with many wonderful doors to walk through, and on the other side is always fulfillment, enlightenment, joy, peace and positive expression of the God Creation Force within you. We want you to see your own futures, bright, beautiful and meaningful. We want you to find that depth of spirit that brings significance to your personal life, whatever that may be for you. We want you to embrace all that you are and all that you will become.

Allow yourself to create wonderful visions of the highest and best future that this earth can manifest. Expand upon those visions, play with them and together, truly dear ones, we can all create a joyful and peaceful reality for all.

CREATING LESSONS OF JOY

In our view, dear ones, you are all majestic beings. You are here to experience the human realm. You are here to learn some lessons, but most of all dear ones, you are here to experience joy. Choose joy to be your greatest lesson in this lifetime: How is it that you can experience more and more and more of it? Know that even amidst the chaos, you are still you, there is still that beautiful spark of light and joy that is inside of you, that is your soul. Your soul knows joy. Your soul knows bliss. Your soul knows the oneness of All That Is.

MEDITATION TO RELEASE THE PAST AND EMBRACE YOUR FUTURE

Set aside some time to meditate. Give yourself the opportunity to release the past and allow the essence or energy of your future come forth. What do you need to release from the past? What is your most perfect future? Have you envisioned yourself living 5 years from now? 10 years? 20 years? Can you even see it? Can you put yourself into the picture? We want you to see your positive essence living forth, living your truth, living in your highest potential.

As you begin your meditation process, allow yourself to feel completely relaxed, as your physical body melts away. As you breathe light into your soul, allow yourself to be enveloped in the energy of love. Feel your higher self fully present and your energy field expanding. In this higher state of consciousness, imagine your spirit is ascending into the heavens, into the interdimensional realms

In this expanded state of awareness, begin to visualize and imagine in your mind's eye, that you are visiting a beautiful healing temple. You may see a temple with large marble columns and graceful steps leading up from a peaceful beach. As you explore this beautiful temple, you find a cozy healing room. It is a place of healing, a sacred space where the energy of God prevails. And in this very sacred place, your guides and your angels come to be with you. Make yourself comfortable there, and open your heart to feel their love for you.

As you have come to this sacred place for healing, your guides and your angels wish to help you to release all that you no longer need. Ask your guides and angels to help you to become aware of what you need to let go of and release into the light.

And you may ask what fear is holding you back that you can now let go of. Even if you can't identify exactly what it is, just see any energy blockages in the body, releasing and pouring forth all that you are ready to let go of.

See it all transform into light as you keep letting it go, releasing.

As you continue to release, your guides and angels wish to share with you their insights and wisdoms, and what lessons have come from this release. Open your third eye and receive those insights and lessons now.

As all these energies that have been released have been transformed, allow yourself to fill in any energy holes left behind with love and positive healing energy. It is time to open your heart and receive, like a pouring in of loving, healing energy into your heart, which then spreads throughout the body to fill every part of your soul with love and peace.

As you fill your body, mind and spirit with love, feel your own self-love coming into wholeness and completeness.

As you step into the fullness of all that you are, your guides, your angels and your own higher self all wish you to know how magnificent and wonderful a being you are. Take a moment to revel in all that you are, breathe into the light, and as you feel the light of all that you are, your guides and angels wish to help you see the new you of the new millennium. Open your psychic vision to see you in a magnificent future. Allow the future vision to unfold.

Allow the feeling, the quality and the essence of your most glorious self to be felt at this time.

Your guides and angels wish to show you a very, very special time that awaits you as you come into the fullness of all that you are. Open and feel that very special time that this new millennium holds for you.

Your guides and angels wish to share with you all the magnificent qualities, the power and the magic that lies within you. Open and allow yourself to see, feel and hear even more of who you are and who you are becoming.

Your guides and angels wish to share a very special gift, perhaps it is a symbol, a word, or a vision, but open to receive a very special gift that will be a tool for your ultimate manifestations. Receive your gift now.

Your angels' and guides' final gift to you is some healing, loving, empowering energy as they open their hearts like the floodgates pouring forth their love for you. Receive that love and gift of empowerment as your own knowledge of the strength within you and the beauty within you.

Fill yourself with all the self-confidence that you need to go forth in your life with your head held high, feeling proud of who you are, honoring the power within you and honoring the Creator within you. Integrate those empowering energies into every cell of your body. And with each breath, breathe in the integration of self-confidence, self-esteem, self-worth and with each breath ground those energies back into your physical body, as you bid your angels and guides a loving farewell for now, knowing that they are always there for you. Gently breathe yourself back into your physical body, retaining all the bliss, the comfort and the power of all that you are.

We send you love as we honor the joy and the beauty of your soul. We are ONE."

CHAPTER 6

HONORING THE GOD WITHIN EVERY DAY

I believe that we are *all* children of God and therefore, we all have a part of God in our hearts and souls. Let's take that concept a step further and consider that our core, our soul, is Divine and that we have the ability to understand, feel and know a God-essence that dwells within us.

How does that God-within play out in our day-to-day lives? We have free will choice, but what about our own Divine intervention? When we are guided by our higher self or gut intuition, is the God-within keeping us on the path to our highest and greatest destiny? What does the higher self or God-within mean to you, personally?

In a recent series of meditation groups ONE spoke of this very subject and led a beautiful guided meditation to help us honor the God-within every day. In this chapter, I will share with you their message and their meditation.

ONE: "Greetings, dear ones. We so often talk about the God-within and your own higher self, but how often do you have that strong sense of knowing, that strong connection, that strong integration with your own higher self? Your day-to-day busyness can sometimes cause you to feel a bit overwhelmed, tired or perhaps distracted. You might feel a longing within your soul that you can't quite place or identify.

We want you to know, dear ones, that this is a time for truly developing an intimate relationship with your higher self. We'd like to talk about that God-Self, that higher self within you; the part of you that is Divine, the part of you that is a Creator, the part of you that knows all, sees all, understands all and has access to the wisdom of the ages. We want you to know, dear ones, that you are so much more than just your physical body, and indeed death is evidence of that because as the body may die, the soul lives on.

Indeed, today we are going to help you access that soul part of yourself with more consciousness than perhaps you have had before. We want you to have an awareness of the soul that dwells within the body. Certainly it is good to have unity of body, mind, and spirit and to feel the oneness of all that you are in your present form. However, remember that in all your other lifetimes you also could experience oneness of body, mind, and spirit with a different body. Even in this lifetime, your body changed and evolved from a baby to an adult, and yet it is the same soul that occupies it. So, dear ones, the oneness is really more about a state of acceptance and honoring and acknowledging of all that you are in your present moment. We want to help you develop this greater intimacy, knowingness and consciousness about your own higher self.

We'd like to begin by explaining to you how it is that we see your soul. We want you to know, dear ones, that you are all indeed divine magical beings. If you take away the physical body what have you got? Well, we see a lightbody. We see you, but it is light. It is not so dense with all of the molecules together like you have in your physical third-dimensional body, but it is a body, a lightbody that is in what you might consider to be the etheric realms, but yet here you are dwelling in the physical realms simultaneously. It is as though the lightbody integrates, merges and finds oneness with the physical body. When you have an awareness that the lightbody (or God-within/higher self) is present within and about the physical body, that is when you are feeling fully integrated, feel your best, and feel the oneness of all that you are.

Of course the lightbody may extend and be larger than your physical body. Meditation will help you amplify the lightbody, to bring more energy into your auric field so that you are actually even bigger and more light than what appears in the physical. You can actually extend your aura to fill the entire room (and beyond) with your lightbody.

When we guide you in meditation, we always bring in the light of God/Goddess/All That Is and ask you to imagine Divine white light filling the room. From our perspective, you all become one with the body of God energy and, indeed, it expands your auras so that your auras all blend as one, one beautiful combination of all your delightful individual energies resonating in the bliss of oneness. Of course it isn't always experienced on a conscious level and understood by each individual that that is what is happening but that is how we see it from our nonphysical perspective.

Dear ones, know as well that when we see your higher self, when we look at you and we see your lightbody, your soul, your spirit, we see a beautiful loving energy pulsating, radiating from the heart chakra. In your lightbody the heart chakra can often glow the brightest and have the most amount of energy flowing around it because truly this is the center of your physical body. It is where the life force pumps and keeps the body going, but more than that the heart, as you know, is the center of love, and truly *love* is the driving force behind the greatest Creator Source energy. The love energy indeed is fuel for the soul.

Know, dear ones, that finding oneness and the bliss of fully experiencing the God-self is simply a matter of acknowledging that it is a part of who you are. From our perspective you are all Gods walking around in these human bodies, playing upon the earth plane and experiencing all that there is to experience here, learning your many lessons that you came here to learn, helping all of those that you came here to help, and finding yourself in those almost comical circumstances from time to time to remind you of your humanness.

Know, dear ones, that you are so much more than your physical body plodding though your day, walking your path. There is a soul in you that needs to be reminded that it is never alone, and that it is always dwelling in the heart of God. Your soul wants to be reminded of its own power, of its presence, of its own purpose.

Taking some time each day to honor your soul with some form spiritual practice can be a wonderful gift you give yourself. We'd like to offer some very simple techniques to help you honor the God within. When you wake up, get yourself out of bed and take some deep breaths. Stand with arms outstretched and say with power and strength: "I welcome the God-within and I honor all that I am." Bring into it all that you are and feel it in your heart center. Let the energy of God-within spread throughout the entire body and feel your body come alive with the energy of your soul, your own spirit. Awaken your spirit along with your physical body and that will give you a wonderful feeling of inner peace to start your day.

Mornings are a wonderful time to take a moment to have a quiet meditation, if that fits into your world. It is also a good time to take a nice walk outside and start your day with some fresh air and with your feet firmly planted upon the earth as you walk and enjoy the beauty of nature that is around you. Actually, anytime during the day, make it a point to take a few moments, take a break and take some deep breaths. If you can, take a walk in nature or sit under a tree and breathe with the rhythm of the earth.

The breath is a source of life for you. Pay attention to your breath at least a few times during the day, and take the time to breathe deep. Let the breath be cleansing and full. Breathing fully can indeed help you live longer. The breath can also be used to accelerate your vibration and to help you achieve higher levels of consciousness and deeper levels of concentration and focus. These deeper levels of meditation can help you to connect with your spirit guides, angels and with your own higher self or God-within. Indeed, dear ones, have fun with this one and play with how the breath can be directed and focused for any intention that you place upon it. It is a powerhouse that is always there for you with every breath you take. Use it.

There are many techniques and rituals that you can incorporate into your every day to honor the God-within. Allow your imagination to help you find your own ways. In the meantime, the following meditation can be practiced to help you find new ways of honoring your higher self.

One of the ways we learn is simply to remember, on a soul level, things that we have known before, in our own past lives. This meditation takes you on a time-travel journey to a past life that you knew and honored God-within.

MEDITATION TO HONOR GOD WITHIN

Begin with the "Four-Step Mediation Process" found at the end of Chapter 2. Visualize the white light of the Creator Source filling the room. Just imagine that the arms of God/Goddess are wrapped around you, nurturing you, holding you and loving you. Feel yourself being completely supported and held in the energy of God/Goddess/All That Is.

In this meditation you are going to blend with your higher self and take a journey... Take some more deep breaths, feeling yourself becoming lighter and lighter, and becoming more aware of the God-Self.

With each breath, feel your lightbody becoming more alive and vibrant. See yourself ascending as your lightbody can soar with wings. You fly! Enjoy the feeling of flight as we soar into the heavens to explore the nonphysical realms.

Feel your soul reaching out and flying through the heavens as we are going on a journey back through time to a magical place, a place you have lived before. There has been a lifetime that you knew God-within, a lifetime of honoring your power. It may be your Egyptian lifetime. Or it may be a lifetime in Atlantis, Lemuria, or some other magical place. Allow your soul to travel back to one of these favorite lifetimes, a lifetime of power, a lifetime of great knowledge, a lifetime of spirit living its fullest.

See the surroundings of this place. Smell the scented air. See the beautiful detail around you and hear the sounds. And in this magical place your spirit guides and angels are coming to join with you as they help you to remember more of who you are.

Your guides and angels and your higher self will show you now an aspect of yourself, a past self, that truly honored the God-within you. Open and see more of who you are by seeing who you have been.

You may see ways of honoring God-within, ways of expressing who you are.

Ask what magic or miracles have you performed.

You may see some of the rituals you have done to honor your spirit. See those rituals now.

And you may see some of the creative ways of play and joyful expression of the joy that is within you, within your soul. See your honoring of the joyful, playful part of you.

Breathe into the spirit and ask your guides and angels to show you how to honor your spirit in this lifetime.

Ask your guides and angels to show you the magic and the miracles you *can* create in this lifetime.

Ask your guides and angels what ritual your higher self would like you to do each day to remind you of the God and Goddess that you are.

Ask your guides and angels and your higher self what form of play and joyful acts can you integrate into your life today, to honor your joyful spirit.

Your guides and angels have one last message for you to help you honor the higher self and the magic and the power within you. Open and receive that message now.

As we honor the higher self and acknowledge all that we are, the higher self begins to find its way back again to blend with the physical body and we give thanks to our guides and angels for helping us to find new way of honoring our spirit. Allow these honorings to come and integrate back to your body.

Take some deep breaths and feel once again the oneness of body, mind, and spirit. Take a moment to feel the joy and the exhilaration of the higher self to have a physical body to dwell in at this time. Remember that the expression of the soul is truly joyful. Allow yourself to gently come back into full consciousness when you are ready, feeling fully alive, fully awake and filled with joy at finding the oneness of all that you are.

ONE wishes to share some thoughts in closing:

ONE: "Allow the soul to sing, to dance, to laugh, and to play and indeed you will know the joy of all that you are. We hope you can feel what we are sharing with you and apply it in your life in whatever way fits for you. Embrace some type of ritual into your life to help you in your appreciation, gratitude and awareness of all that you are, and indeed you will experience more joy.

We hope these messages and meditation have helped you to find ways to honor the goodness and the greatness that is you! We send you our love and blessings as we honor the God within you."

Chapter 7

Expansion and Grounding:
The Higher Self and Earth Self as One

In this chapter, ONE speaks with great passion about spiritual expansion, awareness of the higher self, and the importance of grounding with the Earth. ONE then led a beautiful meditation, using the Great Pyramid at Giza as a place of expansion and integration. I especially loved the use of the Queen's Chamber to honor the divine feminine and the King's Chamber to honor the divine masculine. While most spiritual seekers are familiar with the concept of the higher self (or God self) ONE helped us to understand the importance of honoring our Earth self and integrating that oneness with our higher self.

ONE: "Greetings dear ones! We are the energies of ONE and what a joy to be with you once again! As we come to you from the angelic realm we extend to you our loving healing energies. As we reach out and touch your heart we want you to know how loved you are and how truly a magical being you are. We come to share with you some knowledge and wisdom to help you in your spiritual path, to help you come to know yourself on a deeper and more profound level.

We wish to share with you how you can expand your energies. We speak to you about expansion because this is a time in which the energy vibration frequencies surrounding the Earth are very high. From the Summer Solstice through the Fall Equinox, we are in a time that the Earth is closer to the constellation Sirius. This is a time in which the high vibrational frequencies of the loving Sirians are here to help, to support you in your life in a variety of ways.

What is impacting the earth most strongly now is the energy of **expansion**. While many of you have achieved some level of mastery over your physical reality and have more understandings of your life, physically, emotionally and mentally, this is a time to *expand beyond* the present scope of what you know, to expand into the unknown.

EXPANSION MAY BRING CHANGE

We know that some of you are experiencing change or are in some sort of transformation process. We encourage you to stay strong and centered in your strength and your courage and know that the path that lies before you is one you know you must walk. There is no hiding behind the *old* any longer. There is no hiding behind the masks of "the old you," but rather it is time to merge, as the full self, into your new life.

For those of you who have been able to maintain some form of consistency in your life and have created a sense of peacefulness from your surroundings, and perhaps your are not experiencing chaos and change around you, to those people we say that the expansion then becomes more purely spiritual. For those, there is always the mental and emotional expansion as well. But for those of you who are experiencing physical changes in your life, such as moving, changing careers, or changing partners, whatever it is, we are wanting you to be strong in who you are, and to know that the changes that are coming are necessary. You have been preparing for these changes on the higher levels for quite some time and the ultimate manifestation of your highest and greatest destiny is beginning to pour forth in your life. It is as though you must step upon the train, it is moving, it is time to go. You can't just stand there on the tracks or you might get run over! You must get on board and get on with your life and know that this is time to move. Be all right with that.

For those of you who are perhaps settled, you have your home, your life mate, your career, and you are pretty well set there, then for you the moving train is something else. It is up to each one to define what that is for you, but understand that this moving train is energy, perhaps it is awareness, but most of all dear ones it is expansion. You may be solid, centered and grounded in who you are, and yet there is this whole moving part of you, this higher self that is already journeying into your future. It is as though you must go and catch up to your higher self, and catch up with that destiny that awaits you.

We want you to be fearless in this process dear ones, because it is all good. It is the unfolding of your greatness. It is the unveiling of your highest and greatest potentials that lie before you right now. So be courageous, fear not and know that as you expand your perceptions of what you are able to achieve in this life, it is good to expand your perceptions of what spirit guides are there to assist you. Know that there are many angels, Ascended Masters various God embodiments there to support you.

YOUR HIGHER SELF

Expand your interpretation of your own higher self. What is that higher self of yours? Who is he or she? What are they all about? What is the persona of this higher self? If you could imagine your own God self, the part of you that knows all, sees all, Is all, and is at one with God, what is that part of you like?

We can tell you dear ones, that you are full of light, full of knowledge, and your higher self is full of positive expectation of what lies before you. This higher self knows that there is so much more, more to what you can create, more fulfillment, more satisfaction, more joy, more evolvement, more in your own soul evolution and more in coming to know all that you are. So ask yourself, "What is this higher self? How smart am I, really? How bright? How beautiful? How intense? How wise?" How loving is this higher self of yours?

We encourage you to have that more intimate knowing of all that you are. Come into that oneness with the higher self.

That sense of "Yes, I can own this as a part of who I am and acknowledge that God within is the true self, the true being that I am." Of course, the outward embodiment is also who you are. What you are projecting into your world is how you are choosing to represent yourself here in human form, but you are so much more. We are wanting you to expand into that higher self and to begin to have a tangible sense of what is that higher self. What does he or she look like? It may or may not be the same gender identification as your present human body. It may even be androgynous. It may be a God-self that has no gender specific embodiment. Whatever that God-self is, get to know him or her. Come to know all of that you are. Give it a name if you like, so you can call it in and be consciously aware of your higher self fully present in your body. Even if you just close your eyes for an instant, envision this light body, this higher self, that is actually living here in this physical body of yours. Then take that moment to feel the oneness, to feel that yes, you are all of that.

BE AN AMBASSADOR TO HUMANITY

Indeed dear ones, we are also wanting you to expand your belief in what is possible for humanity. While each one of you is on your path finding more and more of what is for you, what is to be, and what you are meant to create, take your dreams up to a higher level of the collective consciousness of all of humanity. Consider yourself to be an ambassador to humanity, the representative or spokesperson of your species. As such, what is your vision for all of man/womankind? What is your grand, expanded view for this society as a planetary civilization? How do you see the evolution of humanity?

We encourage you to ponder those bigger questions and consider yourself the ambassador of humanity so that you can then begin implementing the grand plans. It is not meant to be a burden that you are solely responsible for the evolution of humanity, of course not, but you must know your part is as real and as valid as any other embodiment on the planet at this time. You are all equals in that regard. You all have the inherent right to *live*, to experience joy and to evolve, and so we encourage you to channel your loving energies of that God self into the collective God self of humanity. Imagine that every human on the planet has a God self and all of these God-selves are linked as a higher consciousness of humanity.

The group collective consciousness of all of humanity needs your positive feeding of energy, your positive contributions of enlightened visions of the evolvement of humanity towards its highest and greatest purposes, for manifestations of peace, of love, of finding the goodness in everyone's heart, and giving people the freedom to let that God self come forward in their lives and create.

Imagine how powerful a society, a world you would create where everyone comes into the full knowingness of their own God-embodiment, where everyone understands that they are Creators of their reality. Understand that for each of you, dear ones, as you come into the awareness of the power of all that you are, that truly you are creating this life, you become magical. You become super-aware of your options, your opportunities and the ways you can create beauty, create profoundness, and create sacredness in all that you do.

TRANSFORMATIONS IN CORPORATE AMERICA

Even in 'Corporate America' you can find opportunities to bring in light. We don't wish to sound unfair, since everyone has light inside their souls, but we know that in a corporate environment there can be an emphasis on physical and mental energies, and a void of emotional and spiritual energies. Many corporate environments need the energy of the heart to bring balance and the energy of the spirit to bring upliftment. The heart can bring love and compassion, but the spirit brings the light, and the spirit brings the 'ah ha!' - the enlightened awarenesses that create expansion.

For those who are in constrictive environments, who may one day be faced with the prospect of losing or otherwise leaving their jobs, we pray that you find your 'ah ha!' moment and know that this would truly create an opportunity to be free of that which no longer serves you. There will be many who will find their life's calling because of this. We praise the higher selves for knowing what is in their greatest destinies.

For those who choose to work in a corporate environment because it serves your purposes well, we honor you as well. Be the shining light of who you are, and know that by staying in your integrity, you teach others. Show your colleagues how to live a balanced life by living your truth. We know that many of you serve humanity in these positions in countless ways. Do not underestimate the many purposes your presence serves.

EMBRACE YOUR ROLES

Understand that many of you will encounter people who will be undergoing some form of change or transformation or chaos, and as you come into the presence of some of these people, understand that you may be called upon to be the healer, to be that clear voice of reason amidst the chaos, to be the truth bearer, the light bringer. Embrace those roles as you come into them and know that truly you are serving that grand consciousness of man/womankind. As you help each one, you are feeding the grand plan. You are feeding the positive energies of manifestations and the ultimate destinies of man/womankind.

Know that there are no small acts of kindness, because each seemingly small act of kindness translates up into the higher realms as being so much more. That is why, dear ones, that when that eventual day comes, way down the road, when you make your ultimate transition into light, there will be countless souls thanking you, filling you with love and gratitude for a kind word, for that boost they needed, for that support, that enlightened perspective, for that look in your eyes that gave them the hope to go on. There are no small acts here, dear ones. Know that as you share love and compassion, truly you transform this planet.

MOTHER EARTH

Know as well dear ones, that Mother Earth is always welcoming of your loving, healing energies. We do not wish to say that Mother Earth is in any danger whatsoever, for she is not. She is more solid than you know. Mother Earth however, is a living breathing being of light. This planet you know as dirt, rock and oceans is so much more in spirit than that which the human consciousness can sometimes comprehend. Your Mother Earth loves you, nurtures you, nourishes you and loves you so much. What a magnificent being she is to host all these billions of people walking upon here all the time and hammering away at her. Imagine a blessed mother surrounded by many many children, all demanding attention, and to the observer it may seem that the children are constantly pestering here, but the mother responds with love. The mother is there, loving all of her children equally. The mother is infinitely loving, patient, kind and nurturing. And so it is that your Mother Earth loves you more than you know. All we ask is that you have the awareness of her, so that you can support her in your love and in your energies, because while you are here you are anchored upon your beloved Mother Earth.

HIGHER SELF AND EARTH SELF AS ONE

While we have discussed your higher self on many occasions, we'd like you to consider another important aspect of who you are, the Earth self. Consider your physical body to be your Earth-self. You are made of the same carbon and water that your Mother Earth is made of. So just as your spirit could be considered as a child of God, hence the God self or higher self, your body is a child of Mother Earth, hence your Earth self. Creating a feeling of oneness between the higher self and the

Earth self can bring a sense of groundedness and balance.

Grounding your Earth self is becoming more important because the energies that are radiating to the Earth now from Sirius, the Ascended Masters, and God-Embodiments, are of very high vibrational frequencies. It can be a time of feeling spacey, perhaps your mind is wandering more, or you may be having more spontaneous moments of psychic awareness. We don't want you to be clumsy in your physical world, tripping yourself up because your head is in the clouds. So we would like to suggest that you practice some form of grounding exercises whenever your think of them, or whenever you think you need them, which is more often than you might think.

Find your oneness with Mother Earth. Feel the common vibrational frequency that you share with Mother Earth. While we are always talking about being aware of the higher self and finding that oneness with God/Goddess/All That Is, and how delightful and blissful that can be, we wish to suggest that you can find that energy of blissfulness but in a grounded way by being at one with Mother Earth. Feel the oneness, feel the massiveness of her and feel her not being separate from you, but that you are rather like an extension of her. Imagine you are like a tree that grows out of the Earth but is still at one with the Earth. Visualize that you are a tree, and that you have your many branches of energies that come out, but that your roots are here in the Earth. So we encourage you, in a visualization, to grow roots that come out of your feet and branch out into the Earth, all the way down to the core the Earth. Imagine that at the core of Mother Earth is her heart. Yes, it is a molten lava center, but that is her heart, the center of her love and passion. See your roots going down, embracing and wrapping around her heart. Feel yourself anchored securely in the Earth. That is a profound technique that we are most joyful to share with you.

There are also ways in which you can breathe energy and groundedness back into your life. Often during the day your breathing may be shallow and that may tend to keep your energies in your upper chakras. We encourage you to breathe deep into your bowels, all the way into the body. Imagine the oxygen coming down through the body. Create a visualization for what oxygen looks like in your body. Perhaps it looks like colors or light. Do not visualize it as bubbles of air, because it might feel physically uncomfortable to think of it that way. Rather, think of it as light and energy. Breath is energy. Take a deep breath in and bring it all the way down to your feet. Imagine that your feet have lungs and you need to have your feet breathing. That is another good visualization for you.

One of the best forms of grounding is walking on the Earth, especially in a beautiful place in nature. If you can't be outdoors and you need grounding, just imagine yourself walking barefoot upon the Earth, whether it be on a sandy beach with the waves lapping at your feet, or in a nice grassy field, or perhaps in a mud pit somewhere, where you can squish the mud between your toes. Yes, have fun with that one! Let it be a joyful experience. Ground the visualization into your body and try to have some physical sensations of interacting with the Earth in some way, whether it be hugging a tree or rolling around in the grass or in the snow. Find the visualizations and imaginations that work for you.

For our beloved kinesthetic friends we encourage you to ground energetically with the Earth. Imagine a strong grounding energy in a darker color, such as a deep burgundy red, or an Earthy brown or a rich forest green. Pick any deep color that resonates with you and fill your body up with that color. Feel what that color feels like in your body. Imagine if you could pack your whole body with mud, how grounding that would feel.

We encourage you to discover what grounding techniques work best for you. Be creative. Work with the body and know that the body must be anchored here, because that is how you will do your greatest work. When you have oneness with Earth and oneness with God simultaneously, that is when you can experience true oneness with your body, mind and spirit.

A MEDITATIVE JOURNEY TO
THE GREAT PYRAMID AT GIZA

Let's begin with our basic four-step meditation process: get comfortable, breathe, invite God and surrender. Welcome in all your loving angels and spirit guides and ask them to raise the vibration of the room to be peaceful and loving.

With each breath, feel yourself becoming filled with more and more light and awaken the higher self within you. Imagine that large column of light coming down from the heart of God, going right through you, down into the core of Mother Earth. Feel this column of white light connecting you to your higher self, and connecting you to God, to your Source, to the All That Is. Open all your chakras to be in receiving mode as you allow the energies of light to permeate you, to surround you, to heal you and balance you. As you bask in the white light from the heart of God, feel your oneness with All That Is.

Now begin to imagine that from the heart of Mother Earth another column of light comes up. Mother Earth's column of light may be white light or may be in an earthy color of light. Whatever it is, feel that column of light coming from the heart, the core of mother Earth, going up through your feet and out the top of your head, all the way up into the heart of God. Feel the love and the energies of Mother Earth coming up and filling you with a very grounded, nurturing energy. Open your heart to feel her love for you, as you simultaneously open and feel the love of God as well. Take a moment to feel the perfect blending of Father God and Mother Earth as one, as you. Once again, feel your oneness with All That Is. Take another moment to feel the infinite potential of all that you are inside of this oneness.

In this heightened state of awareness begin to feel the expansion of all that you are into the All That Is. Feel your multi-dimensionality and feel yourself expanding into the higher realms, into the oneness. For in this expanded state, we are going to journey to a very sacred place in the higher realms. We are going to journey to the Great Pyramid of Giza, which may be an etheric form of the Pyramid in the higher realms. In your mind's eye, begin to imagine yourself journeying now to the one, Great Pyramid. In the higher realms, it is a golden pyramid, radiating a brilliant light, a light of wisdom, of knowledge and of the purity of the God essence.

Now within the Great Pyramid find yourself journeying to the Queen's Chamber. Later we will journey to the King's Chamber, but for now begin to find your way through the passageways leading you to this very sacred space known as the Queen's Chamber. The Queen's Chamber radiates the Divine feminine essence, the Mother Earth essence, the Blessed Mother essence, the Goddess energy. In this Chamber, your spirit guides and angels have come to be with you to share with you an aspect of your spiritual evolvement to help you expand into your own Goddess self. Take some time now in the Queen's Chamber to be with the Goddess/Mother Earth energies and receive your messages of expansiveness.

Feel your oneness with the Goddess/Blessed Mother and Mother Earth as one. Feel the Divine feminine aspect blending with your higher self, to bring you the wisdom and the knowledge that you need now.

As you integrate the Divine feminine aspects within you and integrate the expansiveness that has been given to you, whether conscious or not, gather your soul, your spirit to come and journey now to the King's Chamber, the Grand Chamber of the Divine masculine near the crown of the pyramid. As you begin to journey through the halls, you are drawn to a chamber of great light. You may begin to feel the powerful, magnetic energy of the King's Chamber, a magical and sacred place. As you begin to enter the King's Chamber, come into the awareness that there is a gathering of your spirit guides and angels as well as some Ascended Masters that have come to be with you. For in the King's Chamber you will receive messages, knowledge and even more expansion into all that you are. Take some time now to be with your guides and to receive the knowledge, the wisdom and the expansion that they wish to give you now.

In this magical chamber of light your guides and angels wish to share with you even more about your life's purposes here and the Divinity that is within you. Take some time now to blend with the Divine masculine energies present and open to receive more of the higher wisdoms and the expansion of energies that are meant to be shared with you now.

As you may know at the top of every great pyramid there is a crystalline capstone that is the pinnacle of energy. Your guides and angels wish to present you with an etheric representation of this crystal capstone and place it upon your head to amplify the expansion. Take a moment now to feel the crystal capstone descending upon your head, expanding your connection to all the universe, expanding your awareness to all that you are.

To bring all this into completion, your spirit guides, angels and master teachers wish to offer you a closing message of faith, of belief in yourself, a message of courage, courage to live the life you are meant to live here. Take a few moments to receive your final messages from your guides and angels now.

As you honor and acknowledge the gifts you have received in these sacred Chambers, the gifts of wisdom, expansion, spirit, knowledge and strength, begin once again to visualize a column of light coming down from the heart of God and a column of light coming up from the heart of Mother Earth, anchoring and grounding you back to your Earthly body. Know that you can return to the Great Pyramid at any time in your meditations to continue the work of your spiritual evolution. Return gently and softly back to this time and space, fully aware of the gifts and expansiveness you have received. Anchor the light of the higher self back to the physical body, feeling the oneness with All That Is. Feel fully present, fully alive in the now moment, fully content with the knowledge you have received, knowing that even more may continue to unfold for you in the days to come."

* * * * *

"We encourage you to know that you have infinite wisdoms, infinite intelligences and infinite capacity to heal the heart. Your spirits, dear ones, are so bright, so beautiful, so profound and so loving. We hope you can appreciate all that you are and integrate the oneness of all that you are into your day-to-day life.

That is the essence of our message for you now and we hope you have felt our excitement and our enthusiasm for sharing it with you because this is such a wonderful time for all of you. We hope that you can embrace the opportunities that are coming up and to be completely fearless, that you can go forward in your lives knowing that you are the Creator of your destiny and with that, you can't help but create greatness.

We send you our love and blessings through all time. We are ONE."

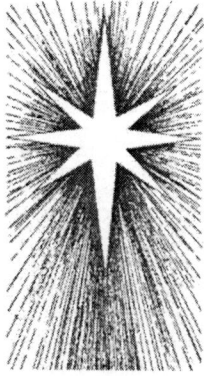

"You, my beloved child, are a part of me.
I am in you and you are in me.
We are one today and for all time.
As you open your heart to me,
you open your heart to all that you are...
and you open the doors of
infinite blessings in your life."

Christ
channeled through Terra Sonora

CHAPTER 8

EXPERIENCING THE CHRISTED SELF

ONE: "Greetings dear ones! We are the Energies of One and indeed it is a joy to be with you once again! This is a time of great expansion, but with more groundedness. Circumstances may still be chaotic for those who resist change, but for those of you who can clearly envision your chosen destiny, a clear path will stretch out before you. Fortunately, you are not alone in this endeavor of life. There are many aspects of God or the Christ that are here to assist you. If you allow the highest energies of God/Goddess/All That Is to blend with you, you can experience your own Christed Self.

WHAT IS YOUR CHRISTED SELF?

We often refer to the higher self as the God-self or the part of you that experiences eternal oneness with God. The higher self is your lightbody. your soul - the part of you that lives beyond the death of the physical body. As we have said before, taking time for meditation will enhance your awareness of your higher self. Practice breathing light or life force energy into your lightbody and gradually you will have a sense of distinction between the physical and non-physical aspects of yourself.

What is the next level of understanding of the higher self? We call it the Christed Self. This is about accepting that you are loved and honored by God, by Christ, as a valued member of their Earth team of humanity. This is about accepting that you are respected by God, even revered for your courage. Can you accept this mantle of honor from God? Can you begin to feel worthy enough of such honor?

To better illustrate this point, we refer to a very sacred event when the Christ spoke through our channel. We will ask that the text of what the Christ said to our channel be inserted here:

"I have come to honor you today." He went on to say, "You, my beloved child are a part of me. I am in you and you are in me. We are one today and for all time. As you open your heart to me, you open your heart to all that you are. I come to you this moment, your own Christed Moment, to open your eyes to the truth of who you are. As you open your heart to me, you open the doors of infinite blessings in your life. Know in your heart that everyone you meet has me inside their hearts as well. See everyone as your father/mother/brother/sister/God and know that we are all one. Share your heart-felt knowing with others that the love of God is in each soul and they too can call forth their own Christed Moment, to allow me to honor their life."

We believe this is a message intended for each member of humanity. While our channel may be unique in her ability to transcribe this message so clearly, it is there for anyone who wishes to connect with the Christ and experience it for themselves.

You become more aware of your Christed Self when you accept the love and honoring that is there for you, and accept the responsibilities of the higher purposes you have come here to fulfill. You live your life in a way that is honoring of the Divine intentions your life will serve. You begin to see your life as a vehicle for serving God and serving humanity.

Many will ask themselves, what purposes do I serve? How can my life have importance or significance in the eyes of God/Goddess? Our response is to ask you if you have loved well. Has your love made a difference in someone's life? Has your kindness and generosity touched someone's heart? Do you live your life in a way that honors life?

Your life's purposes are not intended to be a burden. You can serve God and serve humanity in countless joyful ways. If you follow your bliss you are serving God and humanity.

YOUR LIFE'S PURPOSES

What is the purpose of your life? There are so many answers to that question, that only you will know what is in *your* soul to complete in this lifetime. This is a time of examining the inner you, examining the total you and finding the higher purposes you have come to fulfill. Take some time to really feel what is in your heart. This is a time of feeling the clarity to move forward in the direction of your heart's desires.

Understand, dear ones, that many of you are fulfilling your life purposes in the day-to-day activities of connecting with others. There are no small purposes served in sharing your love, compassion and wisdom with others. However, beyond that, we want you to know of the expansion of awareness inside of you. This expansion is more about your own self image, your self-confidence, your self-esteem, and your self-worth. It's about all of those qualities growing richer and deeper so that you come to understand yourself with a richer and deeper feeling of gratitude. You are learning to appreciate your gifts, your talents, your abilities and you are more open to honoring them.

You are coming in the awareness of how your own creative energies need to be expressed in your world. This is a time that your talents and abilities are coming into fruition, and you are coming into such strong awarenesses that your life's purposes can no longer be denied. This is a time of taking action.

This is also a time to 'Fear NOT!' There is no need to be afraid of anyone. There may be people in your life who are saying 'No you can't!' In spite of whatever challenges may be put in front of you, you must listen, dear ones, to that inner voice that says, 'You are *more*!' It is time to do more, BE more, and you must know, without any self-doubt, that you *are* so much more than what those people with a limited view can now see in you.

Understand that how you define yourself is what is changing now. Begin to accept that you are not the same person that you were in the past. The belief patterns of the "old you" are changing and expanding. What is changing now is your own internal definitions of who you are. It is time to break out of those molds, break free of the old self-imposed limitations and restrictions of what you thought you were capable of doing, and beginning to understand that your soul wants more. To help find what that 'more' is for you, take some time to explore your relationship with God/Goddess/All That Is.

DEFINING YOUR RELATIONSHIP WITH GOD

Think about this for a moment. What is the Creator? What is this God/Goddess/All That Is? As we have come to understand it, it is infinite love, infinite intelligence, infinite wisdom, a Being, if you will, that is all-encompassing, the Source of All that Is, your Creator. The Being that birthed forth your spirit into light.

And so, dear ones, we would want you to come to know your Creator, your Father/Mother/God, and to sit in audience with this God, this Creator, and give it a persona, a likeness that you can relate to. How do you visualize God? Do you see a Father God, or a Mother God/Goddess [Mother Mary, Mother Earth, Elohim]? Perhaps you may see Buddha, Jesus Christ, Great Spirit, Allah, Jehovah, Ra, YHWH, or Krishna. Some may see God as a huge burst of infinite light, like a brilliant thousand million suns of light, but you might have difficulty sitting across the table and talking with that. So bring in a "God embodiment" as we call it, a personification, an embodiment of God that you can relate to. Many choose the Christ. Yes, that wonderful being that walked the Earth as the man Jesus certainly embodied the essence, the love, the purity, the truth, the beauty of your Creator, in human form, specifically so that you could begin to relate [God] to something that you knew. As Christ fully proclaimed himself to be the son of God, he showed each one of you how you are children of God as well. And just as the Christ would happily sit across the table from God the Father and have a chat with him to help himself understand His life purposes, and His reasons for being, we would encourage you to do the same.

A MEDITATION WITH GOD

We wish to offer you a meditation to help you deepen your relationship with the Creator. Indeed, dear ones, this can be a profound experience. We wish to suggest that you take some time for meditation, to sit and be still. Begin the four step meditation process: get comfortable, breathe, invite God and surrender.

Take a moment to feel the presence of your higher self. In that expanded state, call forth and envision the embodiment of God or a Christ that you are comfortable with to be sitting across the table from you. This aspect of God has come to be with you and talk with you today. Ask what God desires for you and your life's purposes. Be completely open that it may not be anything miraculous, or perhaps something that you already know. Just keep an open heart to feel, hear and see the highest and the best hope and dream that the Creator could give to you, and begin to feel and understand what the Creator wishes YOU to experience in this life. How does the Creator see your fulfillment, your satisfaction, and your ultimate joy?

Then in this meditation feel the essence of God or Christ begin to expand and radiate, and blend with you. Feel the loving, healing energy that is there for you. Allow yourself to feel what we call "The Christing." Imagine the Creator declaring the Christing of your soul and feel your own Christed Self awaken. Allow yourself to feel the oneness with these grand and glorious purposes that you are here to fulfill. Feel the oneness of the infinite satisfaction, the infinite fulfillment, the infinite love that you are meant to experience here and allow that oneness to be integrated.

Then allow the honoring. You can begin to open your heart to accept that your God and Christ honor you and your purposes. In your vision, you may even see the Creator or the Christ bowing to you, and some, yes, touching the feet or perhaps kissing the feet, honoring you, adorning you with the mantle of peace and honor that you are here to experience.

EXPANDING YOUR SPIRITUAL AWARENESS

Take the time to do this meditation whenever you are wanting to feel your oneness with God and in alignment with your higher purposes. Another perspective would be to consider that you are not just an isolated fragment, no, but rather you are a key player on God's team. You are here to work in Divine synchronicity with your environment and with the people in your lives. This is a time of connecting with these kindred spirits, the like-minded beings in your life, the people who love, honor and support you, and to feel your oneness with them. When you sit and talk with the Creator, ask what is it that you, as individuals, can come together and create that is so much bigger than what any one of you could create alone. Then work with others for the greater good of all.

These are the types of experiences we want to help you create because we want you to know that you are precious, that your lives are never wasted, and that in the higher realms you are honored and revered. There is something very special that you are here to give. We want you to know that, and we want you to feel confident in those purposes, confident that you have the ability to carry it through. Its not just a hope, dream or wish, but rather it is your course. That is what we want you to experience.

We also want you to know that this is a time for being loving to yourselves. It is a time of making sure you set aside some time just for you. Give yourself that day off. Give yourself that nice walk in the fresh air, feeling the beautiful Earth beneath your feet, smelling the crispness in the air, feeling the gentle breeze upon you and reveling in the beauty of this planet. Appreciate the unique gifts of each season.

We hope that you can take the time to feel how Mother Earth's changes are mirrors of the changes within you. For example, in the Fall you might ask yourself what crusty old leaves are you shedding? There may be some things in your life that have dried up, served their purpose and you are ready to let them go. In the Springtime, you can ask yourself what new creation are you ready to birth into the world? During the times that Mother Earth transforms herself, notice how it is being mirrored as some transformational experiences inside yourself.

Indeed, dear ones, we feel such joy in your lives, such infinite potential for joy that we hope you can feel and know the same. We wish for you the bliss of oneness that comes from embracing your own Christed Self. Our love and blessings to you. We are ONE."

"Whatever your life purposes are,
know that you have some very
special abilities within you to help
bring forth those purposes into their
highest manifestations.
We want you to honor those gifts of
spirit and truly honor the expression
of God/Goddess that is within you.
To integrate this concept
into your life is to create joy
in all that you do."

"ONE"

Chapter 9

Allow More JOY into your Life

ONE is always reminding us that we are here to experience as much joy as we can. Their messages help me to remember that we all have the inherent right to create joy in our lives. Too often I see people who are mostly joyless and who seem to struggle with life itself. My heart truly goes out to those who have challenges in life. It is my hope to help everyone to understand that joy can be an amazing, wonderful part of your life, no matter what your circumstances. Joy is who you are, what you can create, and a lifestyle that you can choose. Please hear "ONE's" words and take them into your heart.

ONE: "Greetings dear ones. Today we wish to speak to you of joy. Know that the most important thing that you can create is joy. Joy can be one of the most miraculous healers of all humanity. Imagine the healing power in the sound of a giggling child. Imagine someone who is depressed or perhaps very ill and they play a tape recording over and over of uncontrollable giggles of children. Can you imagine just how healing that would be? The power of that is so underestimated.

Know, dear ones, that you have that giggling child inside of you at all times. That giggling child inside of you wants to come out and play more and more and more. By allowing the silliness, allowing the humor, and allowing the unabashed fun, you can create miracles in your life and in the lives of others.

The greatest gift that you can give to your own higher self is as much joy as you can stand. Indeed, by doing this, you will make your higher self, your angels and your loved ones happier than you can imagine. Our greatest wish for you, dear ones, is that you push the limit of how much joy you can handle. Some of you can only have so much joy before you put the brakes on. We wish that you would ease off the brakes and that you go for it. Live your life with carefree abandon.

Yes, there is a time and a space for thoughtful responsibility, but you must allow your spirit to be free. Allow your soul to sing, to dance, to laugh and to play and indeed you will know the joy of all that you are. Indeed we hope you can feel what we are sharing with you and apply it in your life in whatever way fits for you. Embrace some type of ritual into your life to help you in your appreciation, gratitude and awareness of all that you are and indeed you will experience more joy.

CREATING JOY

You are blessed to be here in this physical realm with so many pleasures and delights. There is so much joy that can be felt and experienced in this physical plane, that we hope each one of you will pay attention to your inner need for joyfulness and your inner desire to laugh, to share good humor and to share positive, loving, happy energies with others. Bring joy to others, because there are far too many people who are taking their realities far too seriously. We would encourage you to keep your energies centered in love, and bring a bit of light and laughter into the lives of others. We feel this is a timely message for all of you now. Even if this is an intense time for you, we want you to know that this is a time for magical transformations. These intense energies can be utilized in a very positive way to bring all the goodness into your life that you need.

As you choose joy and allow more inner peace, you come into balance with your own soul and you step into the fullness of all that you are. It is then that your life becomes easier. Perspectives seem more clear when you know peace and joy. Know that the love in your heart dwells within you at all times, and that you are never separate from it. Having that knowledge can bring a higher level of contentment and peace that can bring a greater flow of energy in your life. This allows you to move with the energies as they come into your life.

Your spirit guides and angels wish to work closely with you to elevate your energies, and to help you know more of who you are. Call upon them to remind yourself how beautiful and joyful a being you truly are, because they know the power, joy and the beauty that you are.

GOOD FRIENDS ARE LIKE FOOD TO THE SOUL

This new millennium is likely to be a time in which more and more loving and positive people will come into your life. We say that because as you continue to grow and evolve, there is an inward compelling to be with like-minded spirits, to be with positive, loving, supportive people. More and more you will need to honor that and be with people who make you feel good, people who love you, and who give you positive support. This is like food to your soul, dear ones. So give yourself that wonderful treat, go out with that good old friend that you perhaps haven't seen in a while, who makes you feel all warm inside because they love you so much. Go be with those people, treat yourself to some love. Pick up that telephone and make someone's day.

As new people come into your life, love them and be grateful for them. See them as giving you new and interesting opportunities to heal and grow. Give them the gifts of your heart and soul that you are meant to share with them. In turn, love yourself enough to receive the gifts of love and spirit that they wish to give to you.

Be aware that even those people who seem to make your life difficult or challenging, can be viewed as your teachers. What lessons are they giving you? Be aware the time will come when your lesson will be complete and it will be time to move beyond it. Have enough self-love and self-respect to remove yourself from any abusive situations. Thank your teachers for the personal growth and move on. Be aware that the more you love yourself, feel pride in who you are and open your heart to love everyone, the more joyful your life will be.

Our deepest wish for each one of you dear ones, is that you have such a profound level of inner peace, inner strength, inner confidence and self love, that you can carry yourself forward in your life, with your head held high, always wanting to give the love in your heart to all. That is truly a joyful life. We are not speaking of an illusionary life, we are speaking of a true heartfelt life experience, day in and day out.

YOUR SPECIAL GIFTS

Be aware that you have special gifts bestowed upon you by the Creator/Source. These gifts are your own special unique talents and qualities that make you wonderful. We want you to develop those gifts, to acknowledge the goodness and the greatness that is within you that is needing to come forth and be expressed in this world.

It may be that your highest and greatest purposes are simply to be that gentle listener, that soft shoulder that your friend can cry upon when he or she needs it. It may be that your purposes are to heal and to bless others with your loving, healing energy. It may be that your purposes are to teach and to share your wisdoms with all who ask or come to you. Whatever your life purposes are, know that you have some very special abilities within you to help bring forth those purposes into their highest manifestations. We want you to honor those gifts of spirit and truly honor the expression of God/Goddess that is within you. To integrate this concept into your life is to create joy in all that you do.

BREATHING TO CONNECT WITH YOUR HIGHER SELF

The breath can be used to accelerate your vibration, achieve higher levels of consciousness and attain greater concentration and focus. By focusing on the breath, you can reach deeper levels of meditation which will help you to connect with your spirit guides, angels and with your own higher self.

Take some time to visualize your own higher self, you own lightbody. That is who you are. Imagine stepping outside of your physical body a moment and take a look at it. See your higher self. Look it up and down and see your soul. What does your higher self look like? You might even want to give your higher self a special name that you can identify. Call in that name whenever you are wanting to be reminded that you are more than just your physical body.

A JOYFUL WALKING MEDITATION

Take some time to go for a walk, preferably in nature. Take some deep breaths and allow the breath to ground you completely into your body. Breathe with the intention of clearing the mind. With each breath in, use your visualization abilities to see light energy coming into your mind and blowing away all the clouds and the cobwebs. With each breath see more and more of the clarity, imagine or see the blueness of a perfect blue sky, and let that image clear your mind.

As you walk, with more and more clarity of mind and lightness in your step, imagine that your joyful inner child is happy with who you are today. He or she loves you unconditionally and is proud of who you have become. Allow this joyful inner child to be present in your body and move your body in joyful ways. If you are in a public place, this is a way you could certainly spread the joy! Allow laughter and giggles to be a healing balm to your soul. Free yourself from the trap of being too concerned about what other people think. Be yourself and revel in the joy you can create for yourself. As you do this, you can heal on very deep levels, and make a significant contribution to the healing of humanity.

Ponder what activities give you joy. What creates delight and happiness in your life? What playful, fun thing can you do today? Whose life can you impact by sharing your good humor?

Your choices in life can create chaos or create joy. We encourage you to honor your spirit and choose to live your life with a joyous perspective. Regardless of your circumstances, even in the worst of times, the secret to feeling joy is right inside your own heart. Your soul knows joy. Let your soul dance, your heart sing, and your life will be filled with many rich blessings. Our love and joyful blessings to you. We are ONE."

CHAPTER 10

FINDING BALANCE WITH THE ENERGIES OF GIVING AND RECEIVING

ONE: "Greetings dear ones! We are the energies of ONE and indeed what a pleasure to be with you once again! We come to you from the angelic realm as we always do, to share with you our loving, positive healing energies. Tonight, dear ones, our chosen subject is one that is very near and dear to our hearts, which is finding balance with the energies of giving and receiving. The reason this is so important right now is that the energies swirling around the planet at this time are energies of abundance, energies of manifestation, energies of action, and energies of giving and receiving.

While we have spoken in the past about the power of manifesting your dreams and finding your life's purposes, now many of you are out there finally doing it, working your magic and you are finding your right livelihood. You are all taking the steps you need to take to fulfill those dreams and to find that satisfaction. Yet in the process you need to find a sense of balance within yourselves.

This is a powerful time for bringing in more energy. Open up your crown chakra, open up all the chakras, and consider yourself to be a channel of infinite love, light and energy from the universe, so that you do not have to deplete your own energies. In that way, you become more of the vessel, the channel, the vehicle, the conduit for energy to flow through from you to another.

Truly, dear ones, all of your life's purposes can be summarized in a simple concept - its about what you give. Life's purpose is "What do you want to give to this world?" What is it that you wish to flow through you? What is it that you wish to create? Fulfilling your life's purposes is about giving of your soul, your gifts, your talents, your abilities, your magic, to the world. So, in this process, dear ones, its important that you not deplete yourselves, that you not focus all the energy and attention upon giving, giving, giving, but to know when it is that you need to receive.

The secret to finding balance is to know that you are always giving and receiving simultaneously. We hope you can see the truth in that statement. When you give or serve, open up and receive infinite love, energy, support, guidance and encouragement from all of the higher realms, the God realms, the angelic realms, the seraphim realms, and the ascended master realms. All these realms are supporting you and loving you. As long as you stay open and allow yourself to continuously receive, there will never be depletion.

SELF-AWARENESS IS KEY

To live a balanced life, you need to have a keen self-awareness. We know that in your path of spiritual growth and development, you are paying more and more attention to your own needs, desires and your own present state of being. It is important to have heightened levels of self-awareness these days because you need all the information you can get to make your choices lovingly, wisely and appropriate for your highest and greatest good.

Truly, dear ones, making choices for your highest and greatest good can't help but produce the highest and greatest good for all concerned. Indeed, we know that one of Terra's favorite prayers is that she prays for the highest and greatest good of all concerned. That is a good prayer for everyone to use, especially when you are working with energies, when you are working in the subtleties of life.

Specifically, it is important to have the self-awareness of what capacity or mode you are in, in any given moment. Are you in a capacity to give right now? In other words, are you ready and willing to serve another in some way? Be aware of that, because undoubtedly there will be people in your life who will be demanding of you to give. It is part of the dynamics of human relationships. People will often demand energy or attention from you. Of course, many of you do this for a living, so you know well of what we speak.

Whether it is in your interpersonal relationships or in your professional relationships, have the awareness of when you are in a capacity to give. Then open up all the channels of reception, open up the crown chakra, the third eye, the throat, the heart, the solar plexis and ground yourself to Mother Earth with the lower chakras. Open up all these energy centers to help you to have the infinite energy that you need to give endlessly, to give from the heart, and give from a place of strength, a place of confidence and a place of love. Speak your truth from your own higher perspectives and feel your alignment with the energy of God. This way you can give on every level.

Also be aware that there are times, as you know, that you are not in a capacity to give. There are times that you need to shut right down and say "I need some time, some energy and some attention for myself right now." Yes, take the time you need to just kick back, take a hot bath, or go for a walk. Take some deep breaths or go have lunch. Whatever it is, have the awareness of when you need to keep the energy within yourself. Take a moment or two to open up your channels of reception as we mentioned before, but focus that all the energies you bring in, you now keep, and direct the energy to replenish every cell of your body with life, vitality, energy and strength.

You can visualize a very large funnel above your head, with the pure, Divine, loving energy of God/Goddess/All That Is in the form of white, golden or silver light, pouring into the funnel and down into your crown chakra, flowing all the way down into your body. Allow yourself to recharge on every level. As you feel the "All That Is" within you, feel full and content with "All-That-You-Are." This is a recognition of God-within, identical in essence to the "I AM." You can do this in a five-minute break if you need to, or recharge yourself over a whole weekend if you need to. Honor the length of time you need.

WHEN OTHERS DEMAND ATTENTION

When you do that, let's say you have proclaimed your time and space as your own, and someone asks something of you. Now that needy, demanding person shows up in your life again. This may be a family member that you normally give love and attention to. But now they are interrupting "your" time. In this situation, you may need to make the conscious choice of "Yes, I can now open up my energies and allow the energies to flow, to give once again." Then give with the fullness of all that you are, with your heart, your soul and your positive intentions.

We explain this choice because the dysfunctional pattern so many choose to do instead, is to come from a place of anger and snap "What do you want?! You've interrupted my sacred time for me. Go away!" Or something like that, and that is simply not necessary. Rather, it is wiser to have conscious awareness of how you can choose to shift from <u>your</u> space (or state of mind) from <u>receiving</u> to <u>giving</u>. In an instant you can make that a conscious choice. What that does for you, dear ones, is that you never have to give with resentment again. How often have you said "Well, allllllllright... if you insisssttt, ughhhh, but I'm resenting you for this." (Group laughs) Yes, you've all had those times for sure. That can be eliminated dear ones. We share this technique with you because you are in control of your conscious state of awareness. You have the ability to turn on and off your giving and receiving energy at will.

GIVING AND RECEIVING IS SIMULTANEOUS

As we said, the spiritual secret, the higher truth, is that truly you are always giving and receiving simultaneously. It is important to be aware that as you give, you receive. Healers well know this. As a healer is giving a healing session and is channeling healing energy through the hands upon someone's body, the healer undoubtedly receives healing energy simultaneously with the giving. That is a spiritual truth, dear ones. We simply want you to have the awareness of how that simple truth of giving and receiving plays out in all the myriad of scenarios of your life. Apply this truth to your life. Who is it that you give to? Your children? Your spouse? Your customers? Whatever it is, take a look at the dynamics between you and the people you must serve and have that awareness of the giving and receiving of energies. Take delight in the process and choose to create balance in those relationships.

Remember that as you allow yourself to receive from another, you are actually giving them a gift. A gift of gratitude. You know that when you have gone out of your way to help someone or do something special for someone, that you feel so good when they receive with joy. You felt full, and warm and fuzzy inside because you made someone's day. Now, be the one that is receiving the gratitude, and receive that with joy! As you hear "Thank you!" take that loving energy into your heart. Once again the high spiritual truth of giving and receiving simultaneously is proven here.

Have the awareness of that high spiritual truth in your life, that giving and receiving can be of the same energy vibration, and it can be happening simultaneously, constantly in your life. Having the awareness of it can shift you into the energy of gratitude.

THE ENERGY OF GRATITUDE

The capstone to the essence of giving and receiving is the energy of gratitude. It is so important for you to allow the energy of gratitude to have fun in your life, to be present with a joyful quality. Be in the energy of gratitude. Be thankful for the good in your life, thankful for the loving people in your life, thankful for all the abundance of gifts in your life, and the beauty that is around you, thankful for your ability to feed yourself every day, thankful for your beautiful homes, and be thankful for those wonderful people and blessed animals in your life who love you.

To fill yourself with that energy of gratitude, puts you higher to the essence of God. It puts you more in touch with the essence of pure, Divine, unconditional, loving, endless, abundant flowing energy of the universe. The essence of gratitude puts you right in that loop, that constant flow of energy in harmony with the essence of God. Everything is either flowing to or from God and you can imagine all of the energies of the Universe in constant motion. The energy of gratitude plugs you into the abundant flow of All-That-Is. Gratitude plugs you into the essence of freely giving and receiving in an endless flow, an endless loop with the energies of God. You are constantly receiving love and energy from God and you are constantly giving out and serving God through your choices and actions. Enjoy the sacred loop, dear ones. Enjoy the sacred energies of giving, receiving and gratitude because it all ties in with the energies of abundance and prosperity, that there is plenty for all, and that everyone may live an abundant, joyful, gracious and grateful life. Indeed, you all deserve it, dear ones, you do.

ISSUES OF SELF WORTH

If you allow the energies of giving and receiving to flow, it may trigger some issues of self-worth. Even if you have already processed this issue, there may still be some residual old patterns that may come up for you. For example, if someone tries to give you a wonderful gift, there may be a little part of you that says something like "No, I can't accept, I don't deserve this. This is too good a gift for me. You have spent too much money on me. I am not worth that much." Be aware those are all negative programming, old tape loops that you no longer need in your present empowered life. As we like to say, that is a very 1900's sort of thing, that you can leave behind. Yes? In this new century, there is no room for that kind of self-deprecation. There is no room for diminishing your self worth. That has no purpose any longer. It may have helped you at one time to play out a humble role, but it really is not necessary to put yourself down to have humility. What is necessary is that when you are presented with a gift, you must know that that person believes with every fiber of their being that you are well worth it. Take that in. That is part of the receiving. You don't just receive the gift, you receive the intention, the complement, and you receive the honoring. Receive with an open heart and say to yourself "Yes, I am worth it! Thank you!" Feel the delight and the joy in owning your worth, acknowledging your value in their life. That feels so good to us that we hope you can feel the goodness inside yourself and feel the truth of what we speak.

That is the essence of our message to you. We would like to take you on a meditative journey to help you experience the bliss of the energies of giving, receiving and gratitude.

MEDITATION TO THE TEMPLE
OF GIVING AND RECEIVING

Let's begin with our four-step process: get comfortable, breathe, invite God and surrender. Begin to find that deep, still, quiet place within your heart, for today we are going on a journey to a beautiful Atlantean Temple. Let's begin by raising our vibration and feeling the oneness of you and the Creator/Source. Acknowledge the God within and focus your attention upon allowing the breath to continue to relax you. More and more allow that deep peace inside your soul.

Begin to have an awareness of your spirit, the part of you that is light, fully embodied in your own God/Goddess essence. Feel the lightness, the freedom of the nonphysical realms. Today we journey beyond the astral realms, beyond fourth dimension as we ascend into the higher dimensions, fifth dimension and beyond. Feeling the freedom, the lightness, as we journey to a higher plane, to an Atlantean Temple, the Temple of Giving and Receiving.

Begin now to imagine the beauty of this large, open temple, with graceful white columns, water fountains, plants, rich tapestries, tables of fresh vibrant fruits, and candle-lit cozy nooks with overstuffed chairs. It is a place of healing, a place of abundance, and a place of rejuvenating your spirit. Today you are an honored Guest in the Temple of Giving and Receiving. Begin to visualize that within this temple there is a special chair, a throne if you like, that is waiting for you. It is a comfortable chair, one that seems to envelope you in softness, one that is truly meant for a person of importance, such as yourself.

As you settle into your special chair, take a moment to feel the presence of your loving spirit guides and angels, as they come to be with you.

In this place of giving and receiving, you will begin by experiencing the energy of giving.

Imagine now that in this special Temple, the people in your life begin to appear, the higher-self forms of your friends, your family, your loved ones. See their higher selves coming to join with you, with open hearts. Take a moment now to open your heart to feel and know what it is that you wish to give to all of them, whether it be feelings, words, or visions. Give your gifts now to those whom you love.

See them receiving with grateful hearts, fully appreciating you and all that you are.

Now imagine that into the Temple comes the Master Jesus, the Mother Mary, or other God-embodiment, the Ascended Masters and the Essence of God, who all come to be with you.

What is it that you wish to give to them from your heart to theirs?

Feel their hearts open with gratitude, so grateful to you for your willingness to give.

Now with all your loved ones and loving beings of light present, begin to open to what is in your heart, that you are wanting to give to humanity. Everyone is there to help you to know your life's purposes. In this magical Temple, take time now to see, to feel and to know what it is that you are meant to give to humanity.

Imagine all of humanity with hearts open to receiving from you. Feel the essence and the beauty of your gifts.

As this is the Temple of Giving and Receiving, it is time to acknowledge that you have given much, and as time goes on you will give even more, but now you must open to Receive, and to allow the balance.

We will begin by opening to receive from all your loved ones. As the higher selves of your family, your friends and your loved ones step forward, honor that now they have come to give you their gifts, their love and their support. You honor them by allowing yourself to receive with an open heart. Take a moment and receive their love and gifts for you.

Feel your worthiness to receive with love.

Allow the energy of gratitude to fill you, for all the love and support that is there for you.

Now once again, see the Master Jesus, the Mother Mary, all the Ascended Masters, your angels and spirit guides, and the Essence of God, who now come to bestow gifts upon you. Gifts of love or support, which may come as a feeling, a thought, a vision, or sacred objects. Open now and truly receive your Divine gifts from the Essence of God in all its various forms.

Open your heart and receive even more, fully aware that you are worthy to receive these loving blessings pouring forth from the heart of God.

Feel their appreciation and gratitude for you. Let that be another gift you receive into your heart.

Take a moment to bask in the glory of the oneness of All that Is, as you and Christ and all the Ascended Masters blend as one in the energy of bliss.

Acknowledge that your energies of Giving and Receiving are in perfect balance as you feel the flow of giving, receiving and gratitude. Feel those energies swirling around, giving, receiving and gratitude. Feel the flow, the movement of those energies, and feel yourself moving with those energies. As you allow this flow to be felt on every level, consciously choose to always have this awareness of the moving energy of giving and receiving in perfect balance and perfect harmony in your life. Visualize now how these energies of giving, receiving and gratitude, flow easily and effortlessly in your life.

Begin to integrate these energies of giving, receiving and gratitude back into the body. As we say farewell for now to our Temple of Giving and Receiving, please know that you may return there at any time to give, to receive, to feel gratitude and to find balance. Begin now to anchor the balanced energy of body, mind and spirit as one.

Anchor in the energies of gratitude as you once again feel your gratitude to all the beings of light and God-embodiments who joined with you today, for sharing their love and blessings to you. Open your heart to receive their gratitude for all that you are.

Anchor these energies of gratitude back to the physical body. Take some deep breaths and when you are ready, return to the current time and space, to the now, feeling full of love, full of gratitude and clear on your gifts to this world. Be here now, in perfect balance with true inner peace.

CONCLUSION

We want all of you to receive abundantly and to receive with infinite joy. Also, give abundantly and give with infinite joy. That truly makes you so much closer to the essence of God consciously, for you are always close to the essence of God, there is no question there, but being in the conscious loop of it all is a joyful experience. Farewell for now, dear ones. Our love and blessings to you. We are ONE."

CHAPTER 11

FINDING YOUR SOUL FAMILY...
OR BIRDS OF A FEATHER, FLOCK TOGETHER!

I have come to understand that everyone has a soul family in the non-physical realms that may or may not have any connection to your biological family. Your soul family could go all the way back to the beginning - when your soul was created by the Creator. Just as identical twins would share a similar energy, the souls that burst forth from the Creator reconnect in oneness more easily.

I've felt extremely blessed to come to know and love my soul family, which is ONE, the wonderful beings of light that I channel. I know without question that when my physical body passes on that I will ascend into the heavens and be at one with ONE. We will blend with the essence of God and feel the bliss of the oneness of All That Is.

I have felt that bliss and know well the intense love in the heart of God. I wish everyone could have that same inner sense of knowing the essence of God-love within themselves. Then truly there would be no fear of death.

I believe that everyone has a soul family that loves them very much. Some of your soul family may be physically incarnate with you and some may be in the higher realms, acting as spirit guides for those who are living on the Earth now. Please enjoy ONE's insights about soul families, and their incredible guided meditation to help you find your soul family.

ONE: "Greetings everyone! This is indeed a very special time to be alive and so we are most happy to share some information about soul families with you. We'd also like to take you on a guided meditation to help you find your soul family. This is a very wonderful subject that's very near and dear to our hearts as you know, because we are the soul family for Terra and for many others as well.

YOUR MULTI-DIMENSIONALITY

Indeed, dear ones, know that you all have many spirit guides and angels that are here helping you from the other side of awareness or the other side of your third dimension. Please know that all the dimensions exist simultaneously, all intertwined. You can be multi-dimensional, dear ones. You can be third dimensional, fourth dimensional, fifth dimensional, pick a number. You can have any dimension of awareness that you wish, simultaneously with any other number dimension that you wish. The numbers can sometimes put limited definitions upon the unlimited. Our hope is not to overwhelm or confuse you, but rather to expand your awarenesses of how many levels you can exist upon simultaneously.

With that awareness you can begin to experience shifts in consciousness merely by shifting your awareness to what plane of existence you wish to focus your energies and attention upon. In meditation you can set aside some time and sacred space for yourself. Sit for a moment and bring in some white light to expand your consciousness. That is when you have the opportunity to experience more of who you are. In that process, as in the meditation that follows, we hope that you can not only expand your awareness of who you are, but expand your awareness of all the loving guides and helpers that are always there for you.

WHO IS YOUR SOUL FAMILY?

It is our intention to help you come to know your soul family and to strengthen your connection with them. We want to help you feel more connected with more beings of light. Imagine for a moment that in the non-physical realms there is a group of souls that have incarnated with you lifetime after life-time after lifetime. Indeed some of them may be physically incarnate with you in this lifetime. There are some people in your life that you just can't help but feel that you are brother or sister to, some people in your life that you can't help but love with all of your heart and soul. Some of these people in your life may very well be part of that which you would call your soul family.

Keep in mind that soul families are not so rigidly defined that you can't welcome souls into your soul family at any time. Some souls may have more than one soul family, as there can be many overlays. We want you to be open to knowing that there are individuals and groups of souls that absolutely adore you, who think that you are one of the most magical people on this planet, and who truly know your soul. It is like you are one of them. The heart that is within your soul beats the same as their heart. There is a sameness of energy, a sameness of spirit, a sameness of purpose.

Through this connection, this sameness, this oneness, you can feel so much bigger than just what you might think of as just *you*, now. If you can begin to open and see that perhaps you are not just one, but perhaps you are 77 or perhaps you are a hundred, or perhaps you are actually part of a thousand. Open to feel what that is for you. Each one may have different expe-riences, different structures of soul families, and any mix of physically incarnate beings and nonphysical light beings.

We recently met a wonderful loving woman, whose soul family consisted of women. It was quite interesting, we hadn't seen too many of those before, but it was a feminine energy family that embodied the Goddess essence. You may have a soul family that may feel slightly more feminine or slightly more masculine or perhaps it is a perfect balance of both. Perhaps you can all bask in the androgyny of oneness.

Your soul family may feel like a group of earth-centered beings, or a group of angels, or extra-terrestrials, or a simple body of light, just an energy, a fun and loving ball of energy. You may get a sense of a strong heritage, such as Native American, Celtic, Atlantean or Egyptian. You may also get a sense of a cosmic heritage. Perhaps you and your soul family resonate with the energies of the Sirians, the Pleiadians, the Arcturians or other galactic soul families. Whatever it may be for you, be alright with that, and be open to exploring the different aspects of your soul family.

We, as ONE, are a collective, a group of approximately 100 souls. We dwell in oneness you might say, but our soul fragments still have the ability to individuate as we choose. Terra has channeled a being we'll call "One of ONE." This individual or fragment of our soul grouping, expresses a joyful personality and specifically individuated to give Terra a personal message of remembrance of a particular past life they shared together. And so it is that your spirit guide, or your guardian angel might very well be "one of one" of your soul grouping, your soul family. You might think of your life now as "one of many" or an aspect of the group soul that has individuated into this incarnation. We hope this concept can help you feel the power that is behind you in this lifetime.

ONENESS WITH GOD

On another level, we can take this to an even higher concept. For a moment, think of your own higher self as being a body of Divine light energy. Merge consciously with your higher self and then blend energies with your soul family. You become an even more immense body of Divine light energy, and you will feel the oneness. This is sometimes called the over-soul. Some think of the oversoul as the higher self of the higher self, which is always consciously at one with God.

Be aware that you are always at one with God/Goddess/All That Is. You can experience various levels of intensity and various levels of awareness of your oneness with God. As you blend with your oversoul and be at one with your soul family, it is not a very big step from there to feel the oneness with God/Goddess/All That Is. Indeed, some would say it's the same. Think of your soul family as the family of God, if you like, because truly you are all one with God. We are all one with the same family. We can see all soul families merging, blending, and connecting. Indeed, *that* is the bliss of oneness with All That Is.

We hope that some of these insights will expand your consciousness to know that you are never alone here, that you are always part of something greater. You are always one with All That Is. We hope that in the following meditation you can connect on some level with that bigger part of yourself. Our intention is to help you access deeper levels of your own soul that will always be with you and will always be available to give you support, comfort, love, self-awareness and to help you truly know who you are.

MEDITATION TO FIND YOUR SOUL FAMILY

Begin with our basic meditation process: get comfortable, breathe, invite God and surrender. Let yourself come gently into a place of peacefulness, a place of total relaxation. As you let the body rest, let the mind rest as well.

Visualize a beautiful, sparkling white light coming from the heart of God/Goddess/All That Is and feel your higher self merging with this light. We set our intention to go on a meditative journey in our light body to find our soul family and to connect with that Divine oversoul.

As you begin this journey, imagine that you are able to transcend the dimensions, and ascend to the higher realms. For in your light body, you can fly, you can dance and feel the joy of all that you are. Soon you will begin to feel that you are not flying alone. Your spirit guides and your angels are with you all the way.

Open your heart to feel their love for you and let them guide you to a magical place. It is a place that your soul calls home. And as you feel the call, the pull, let the magnet pull you home. Find this place. It is a beautiful place. Feel its energies sing of love. As you find this place you begin to see the details, the vision or the feeling of this, your soul's home. And as you come to land upon this place, you feel comfortable and completely at peace. For truly your heart has found home, and one by one, they begin to gather, your soul family is welcoming you home. It is like being in the center of the universe, the center of your universe. Take some time now to blend with your soul family, to feel their love and support for you, to feel the sameness, to bask in the oneness.

As you connect with more and more of your soul family, you may wish to ask them why they are your soul family, what link or connection do you share, what sameness do you share with your soul family. Open and feel that oneness.

Expand your awareness and feel the realm that you are in. Does your soul family dwell in the Earth realm, the angelic realm, the celestial realm, the cosmic realm, or another realm? Get a sense of where is home for you.

Open to receive the gifts of love that your soul family has to give you. It may be a message, a vision, a word, a feeling or a sacred symbol. Take a moment and receive your gifts now.

Begin to imagine that your soul family, who loves you so much, is linked to an even greater soul family, the family of God. As you blend in oneness with your soul family, allow your entire oversoul to ascend even higher and blend into the heart of God/Goddess/All That Is. Feel yourself at one with all the soul families of the universe. Extend your vibrations into the oneness of All That Is.

In this pure bliss state, open to receive messages or energies directly from God, that relate to your life's purposes here. Receive your Divinity now.

Lastly, your soul family wants to remind you just how loved and special you are. Open your heart and receive their final messages, their final infusion of love energy so that you know with certainty that you are never alone. Hear and feel their commitment to eternity to be with you. Your soul family wants you to know that you can always return home, that home is but a consciousness, an awareness, an acknowledging that you are more, so much more, than your physical body.

As your soul family continues to blend with you, they wish to very gently return you to the physical body that you currently call home. Although you have many homes, you are always home in the heart of God. You are home in the heart of your soul family and you are home in the heart of your own soul. Allow yourself to gently float back, back to the present moment, back to this time and space.

As you breathe deeply you integrate the consciousness of your soul family back into your physical body, integrating and acknowledging all that you have and all that you are. When you feel complete, be fully present, keeping that love, that oneness, that bliss tucked inside your heart. Know that you are so loved. We are ONE."

CHAPTER 12

THE COSMIC ENERGIES OF MANIFESTATION

ONE: "Greetings dear ones! What a pleasure it is to be with you once again. Indeed, this is an exciting time for you, a time ripe with the cosmic energies of manifestation. This is a time to be clear on what you want to create in your lives.

You have come through a process of transitioning into the new millennium energies. You have cleared out the old patterns of the past, and you have worked through the chaos and the fears that have come up for you. You have done all this work to allow more dynamic and creative energy to flow in your life. Now, dear ones, you are truly ready to set your course.

This is a time that you can get the clarity that may have evaded you in the past. This is a time that the energies of certainty can fill every fiber of your being with a sense of "YES! Now I know what it is that I must do!"

In the mediation that follows, we would like offer a powerful tool for you. We will journey to a place, that you create in your mind, a visualization of a magical land of manifestation. You may know the place, some call it fifth dimensional reality or the causal plane. You can ascend into the body of your own higher self and go into a higher dimension where you can create. You step into your own "Creator skin" when you ascend into your higher self. You become more aware of your capacity as a Creator.

THE LIFE YOU HAVE DREAMED OF

We, and your own spirit guides and angels, want to help you, in your manifestation work, to achieve the life you have always dreamed of. Perhaps you are already living the life you dreamed of five years ago. Perhaps you have achieved many of your goals already. But as you well know, there is always more. There is always a higher level of personal satisfaction and fulfillment. There are always more people that you can help, more lives you can touch, more services that you can provide to humanity, and always, dear ones, more and more joy you can experience while you are here in physical form.

Believe in your ability to create the life you have dreamed of. If some of those dreams seem quite huge, don't let that frighten you. Don't let that prevent you from taking the steps you need to take to achieve those dreams. Be aware that not all of you are meant to climb Mount Everest. Perhaps you are meant to be a gentle healer, a gentle teacher, a gentle leader, a gentle inspiration for others. Whatever it is, in your heart you know your life's purposes, you know why you are here. Take time to contemplate your life's purposes. What are your magical gifts and talents that are meant to be shared?

Allow the energies of giving and receiving to flow in your life. There are infinite energies of love, wisdom and intelligence available to you at all times. Allow yourself to be a channel of that infinite love to others. Understand the value of all that you are and all that you give. As you honor the magical presence within you, you will inspire many.

Many of you are branching out. Many have stayed on a steady path. Even if you are on a steady path of spiritual growth and development, you are many-faceted and multi-talented. There are so many things that you can do. The vast array of choices and opportunities may at times seem overwhelming to you. This is a time to branch out, time to step out of that comfort zone that you have created for yourself. It is time to be brave, and take those little risks that can often bear so much fruit and give you so much reward in the future. Don't be afraid to try something new. Feel confident in your ability to succeed at whatever you set your mind and actions to.

THE CREATOR WITHIN

You are as powerful as you are willing to admit to yourself. Some of you may be afraid of owning too much power. But dear ones, that power is awakening within you whether you like it or not. You are stepping into the powerful magician that you are. You are becoming that magic maker, the powerful Creator that you have always been inside of yourself.

The Creator within is finally emerging in more outward physical manifestations because the confidence is growing within you. Your sense of self is growing stronger, dear ones. We have seen so much growth in all of our loving friends. We have seen your confidence levels soar, and we are so proud of all of you. We have seen you more willing than ever before to wear your Creator suit. We hear your higher selves proclaim "Yes! I am the Creator that I am!" Be proud of yourselves, dear ones, acknowledge the growth, proclaim the power, and proclaim the beauty of all that you are.

A TIME OF CREATIVE FREEDOM

This is a very creative time for everyone. Try to set aside some time to allow the free flow of ideas from your spirit to come into your consciousness. Brainstorm alone or with others and write down, or otherwise birth into physical form, the energy impulses of your spirit.

Allow the creative energy to flow through you. There are many who get a creative thought and instantly tuck it away, perhaps for a rainy day. "Yes, I will create that wonderful project, someday, when I have time." How often have you had that thought? Dear ones, know that that rainy day is here, it was yesterday. It is time to get into those creative projects that have sat on the shelf far too long.

This is a time to be free, a time of no limitations, and no obstacles. This is a time to know that no one else has control over you. Any belief that someone has control over you is a false old perception. It is time to own all that you are. It is time to try new things. Your soul needs to experience that sense of freedom.

THE ENERGIES OF CLARITY

Know as well that the energies of clarity are here. You can now sift through those details of life with swiftness and with ease. You will more and more have a sense of "This is important and this is not." "This is the direction I need to go." "This is what I want to accomplish right now." With that level of clarity everything just opens up for you, as though the energies of the universe begin orchestrating the plan. Suddenly the missing piece of the puzzle appears. The universe responds to your clarity with "Here is the person or thing you were looking for" and all the elements and circumstances can come together for you. Allow a new and deeper level of clarity to be present within you.

See your universe as a syncronistic machine at your disposal — that you are the one commanding your universe to bring all the elements of manifestation together so that you can create exactly what you want. If there are obstacles, minimize them. Absolutely, do not give them energies of importance. "Oh that... not a problem." Go around it, hop over it or be the bulldozer and plow right through it. Nothing can stop you unless you allow it to stop you.

Even if you still have your chaotic moments, accept the growth you have earned, and allow a lighter feeling inside yourself to prevail. You have come far enough in life that you can more easily see the humor in your life situations. Know that whatever comes your way, you are able to process your life issues easier with time.

THE CREATOR AND THE HUMAN AS ONE

So, dear ones, you have an interesting challenge of being these magnificent Creators, who happen to be dwelling in human bodies at the moment. So revel in your human-ness, dear ones. Enjoy all of the physical pleasures that are available to you. As the warm weather is upon you, be sure you treat yourself to moments or hours outside in the sunlight, amidst the trees, the grass, the rocks and the water. Soak in the beauty and wonder of nature.

Mother Earth is there to rejuvenate you, to heal you, to provide you with energy and loving, nurturing support. Open your heart to receive her love. Open your upper chakras as well to receive more of the Divine Creative Force and feel that perfect blending of the Earth Energy, which honors your human-ness and the God energy which honors your light body. Feel that perfect blending of masculine and feminine energies, that perfect blending of human self and God-self as One. Feel the joy and the perfection in all of that.

MANIFESTATION MEDITATION

Take some time out of your day, just for you. Yes, you certainly deserve it! Get comfortable, breathe, invite God and surrender. Feel every inch of your body relax as you become a receiver of light, an open vessel, as you fill yourself more and more with the essence of God/Goddess/All That Is.

As you breathe into the essence of God-within, imagine that you have wings of light and that you have the ability to travel to a world beyond this dimension. Begin to visualize a beautiful rainbow that lies before you. A perfect rainbow of multi-colors. See the red, the orange, the yellow fading into green, green fading to blue, and blue fading to purple. As you feel and see this sparkling rainbow of light, imagine that it is your rainbow pathway to a magical land. Follow the arc and journey along the brilliant colors, and feel the healing energy of the colors all around you.

This rainbow is your portal, your interdimensional highway, for today we journey to a magical land of manifes-tation. As you descend down the other side of the rainbow, you begin to see a beautiful land before you. Imagine this magical place of immense beauty. You may see a beautiful crystal castle or perhaps a beautiful landscape in nature. Know that this is a causal plane, a place that as you think it, it is so. Take a moment to familiarize yourself with this magical land. See the details, hear the sounds around you, smell the beautiful scent in the air, and feel the magical energies of your sacred place, your magical land of manifestation.

Imagine that in this fifth dimensional reality, out of time and space, your spirit guides and your angels come to be with you. They come to love you and to create with you. Within your magical land you may see a special room or a clearing. Go there and create now in your mind's eye a *Circle of Manifestation*, with all your guides, your angels, and the ascended masters that have come to assist you. In this Circle of Manifestation, you and the other light beings create a powerful, swirling vortex of energy. Take a moment now to feel the energy of your magical circle, and to be with your guides and angels. Feel the Creator energy all around you.

In this powerful vortex of energy, your guides and angels wish to share with you some messages to help you in formulating your visions, your truth, your knowing of your heart's desire. What do you wish to create in this life? Take some time to call forth from your soul the essence of your deepest heart's desires.

Now your spirit guides, angels and master teachers join energies with you to begin formulating the picture, the essence and the qualities of what you wish to create in this calendar year. Your guides and angels help you transcend time and deliver the energies of your heart's desires to this entire year. See the visions, hear the words, and begin to create in the center of your power circle the manifestations you wish to create this year. See the energy in the circle growing stronger, circulating around the manifestations, giving them energy.

Now your spirit guides and angels wish to move you through the time line to any year you choose, whether it be two, five, nine or fifteen years. Allow your guides to take you through the time line. As you journey through the dimensions, your guides will guide you to a time, a year of significance for you. As you move those energies forward, you invoke your own future self to come and join your circle. Begin now to create a new vision, your future vision, the essence, the qualities, and the physical manifestations from your heart into your physical reality.

As your vortex of energy in the middle of your circle grows and is amplified with Creator/Source energy, see, feel and hear now the manifestation of your dreams, in your year to come.

Your guides and angels wish to add a surprise element to your future. Take a moment to open and receive the essence or vision of another joyful manifestation, out of the blue, that would be a gift from the universe to you.

Take a moment now to feel the joy, the satisfaction, and the qualities of fulfillment. Feel the pride in all that you are and all that you have.

Now begin to visualize that this *Circle of Manifestation*, this vortex of energy that you have created, begins to swirl around, gathering strength, like a cyclone of energy, building with Creator force. Imagine this cyclone then begins to spin tighter, more concentrated, and drawing to you like a magnet. Bring this vortex of energy into you and integrate its power inside of you. As you integrate all the Creation energies, all the manifestations of your futures, all the dreams, all the possibilities, lock in that cyclone of energy to your physical body.

As you anchor your higher self back to your physical body, blending dimensions, fifth, fourth and third as one, feel the integration of your multi-dimensional self, fully empowered in your physical body, totally alive on every level. Take one last moment with your guides and angels to receive the energies that you need right now, receive the words of encouragement, and the final visions of the strength of all that you are. Your guides may have a positive affirmation for you or create one in your mind that feels right for you now.

In completion, there is always an exchange of gratitude and love between you and your guides and angels. As they share their love and blessings with you, they remind you that you can return to your magical land of manifestation at any time, and that they are always there for you, helping you, guiding you, for the manifestations of your highest and greatest destinies.

Breathe deeply and anchor the energies back into the physical. Bring the energy down to your toes. Bring yourself more and more back to the here and now, feeling fully alive, fully refreshed and empowered with all that you are.

May you share with others the greatness that is within you, so that all may know the shining star of your soul. Our love to you, dear ones. We are ONE."

CHAPTER 13

LIVING IN YOUR POWER

ONE: "Greetings! We are the Energies of ONE and what a pleasure to be with you once again! We are excited to talk to you about one of our favorite subjects, living in your power. You are all coming into your power more strongly than ever before. You are coming into a greater knowing of what is inside of you and what it is that must come forth.

DO NOT FEAR YOUR POWER

Living in your power can sometimes feel like you are living with your insides turned out, so that everyone can see what is inside of you. That can be a frightening thing if you think of it that way. It may seem like you are exposing yourself, exposing your truth and your vulnerabilities, and yet, as we perceive it dear ones, living in your power is about standing in your truth, not being afraid to speak that which you know to be true. Be the observer of life, the one who is there to witness what is happening in your world and speak what it is that you see.

In the past, dear ones, there were times that you felt the power of All That You Are,* it may have been a fleeting moment, but you have felt that power. It may have frightened you because all that power can be overwhelming, or you could have the felt the potential of overwhelming someone else. All of you have had the experience of being overwhelmed by someone in the past, and you didn't like that much, so you are not wanting to become the thing you despised.

* We often refer to God/Goddess as "All That Is." Similarly, we refer to your physical self in oneness with your Higher-Self/God-Self as "All That You Are." This is the Divine essence of your soul in your human form.

So many of you hid from your power because that was easier. But that was then, dear ones. Now the energies are such that you can step into the power of all that you are without fear. This is because now your power is specifically intended for, and is very focused on, the greater good of all. It just is. So there can't be any mistakes with your power.

ALLOW THE CHANGES THAT YOUR POWER CAN BRING

As you let go of the fear and step into the fullness of All That You Are, fearless, there becomes this transformation inside of you that is profound and remarkable. That is the change that we are seeing and feeling in you. It is miraculous, dear ones. You have come so far and yet, that power can certainly bring about a bit of discomfort, especially to those who were used to the old you. Those who were used to perhaps shoving you around a little bit here and there, and that simply can't be anymore. You must stand solid on both feet, solidly in who you are. Yes, there is a time to budge when it is time to budge, but we are talking about being strong and being sure - knowing your truth and not being afraid to speak it, live it, and be it.

Acknowledge the changes that are occurring within you. You are growing, dear ones, you are expanding, and you have outgrown the old patterns that no longer work for you. Even if you have been resistant to looking at your issues or facing what is really going on inside of you, we feel that now you can't help but see your life for what your life truly is. It is as though the blinders have come off and now you are looking at your reality, your life with crystal clear glasses. It's as if you've always had the wrong prescription for your glasses, and now you suddenly have the good prescription, and now everything is finally crystal clear. Now you can see your life with a clarity that perhaps was not even possible in the past.

This is because the illusions are falling away. You have recognized your issues and now you are clearly in a phase of doing something about it. You now know what is acceptable in your life and you also have clarity about what is unacceptable in your life. You can make your choices and move forward. With this level of clarity that you are able to experience now, there is no risk of making a wrong decision now. It is more important to make a decision, to make positive loving choices for yourself, and move forward in your life with positive expectation, knowing that you have already let go of the old patterns that no longer suit you. We feel more and more of you are stepping into the fullness of All That You Are - the "I AM"- and stepping into owning your power.

STAY IN YOUR POWER WITH SELF LOVE AND COMPASSION FOR OTHERS

Being in your power is also about feeling good about yourself, having so much self-love, self-respect, self-confidence, and self-esteem that you can go through your life with your head held high, without having that self-talk that can undermine you at times, self-talk that questions your abilities or talents. It is time to silence that voice, or acknowledge its presence and ask it to please be quiet for it is no longer needed in your life. There may have been times in your past that having self-doubt served you in ways of allowing you to be vulnerable at times, and creating lessons for you at the time. But what we feel, dear ones, is that the energies of this new millennium are creating for you new opportunities to stand tall, stand firm in what you know to be true, and to feel so good about yourself that other people can't shake you up as they may have done in the past.

When you are in that position of power within yourself, you teach others by example how to stand in their power. What a remarkable planet this would be if every human being stepped into that power with the grace and beauty that you do. That's so important now, dear ones. As you grow and step into the All That You Are, changes occur within you and you begin to respond to your world differently - not from a position of fear, or uncertainty, but from a position of confidence.

Your new found power may shake, rattle and roll some of the people around you, but it's alright. It doesn't mean that it is time for you to go back to the old way of being, because you can't. Just as the one year old learns how to walk you can't take that away from him or her because you can't make them go back to crawling. That's how you are dear ones, once you step into that power, no one can take it away from you. You can choose to relinquish it when it's convenient, yes; but know dear ones, you can have this power without any harm to anyone. Others will get it, they will figure it out. They will come along and step into their own power so that they can see you eye to eye.

OTHERS WILL RESPOND TO YOUR POWER IN DIFFERENT WAYS

It's important to know that in being All That You Are, others may feel your energy and respond in a way that triggers their issues. They may see the glory, the beauty, the power and strength of All That You Are and may compare themselves.

In their own mind they come up short, and suddenly they are hanging their head down and not feeling as good about themselves. Understand that just as the Christ walked in his power and touched and transformed the lives of everyone that He met, so too, will you.

If your power, your presence, triggers an uncomfortableness in someone else, understand that it is brought up as a gift to them to learn, to evolve, to grow, and to move beyond it. If you see this happening to anyone in your life, lift them up with compassion, and let them see into your eyes and let them see that you honor the God within them as well, that you honor the power, the greatness and the beauty of All That They Are. Lift them up so that you are now looking at each other eye to eye and honoring each other. That is how we see the transformation of this planet, dear ones. Just imagine if everyone does that, where you just lift up everyone you meet and see eye to eye, God to God, honoring of one another. This is the essence of the old Sanskrit word "Namaste" which means the God within me honors the God within you. That is the rite of passage, dear ones. That is the awareness, the acknowledgment of All That You Are and All That everyone else Is as well.

If you find that there are some people in your life who challenge you, on a higher level come to thank them for the lessons they bring to you, for the strength that they well up inside of you. For others do not need to create weakness in you, but strength. Indeed, dear ones, it is important to know when it is that you are being scammed. There are people who will try to scam or deceive you, or attempt to take your power away from you by undermining your self-confidence by their underhanded comments that tell you that you are "less than" they are. It's simply not truth, dear ones. That is all part of the scamming that humans do to one another from time to time in this game of manipulation, of power and control. So, dear ones, have the awareness of when someone is playing these games with you so that you can recognize it, detach emotionally from it, and say to yourself "Aha, there's that game playing going on again. Well, I can buy into it and let my buttons be pushed and be pushed around, or I can choose to stay centered in what I know to be true and not let it hurt me, and not let it have any effect upon me whatsoever." Indeed, dear ones, we are wanting you to have that keen awareness of other people's dramas that can try to pull you in from time to time. Be aware of when that is happening and have the sense of strength inside yourself to set your boundaries where you need to.

YOUR OWN DIVINE ROAD MAP
TO LIVING IN YOUR POWER

This is a time as well, dear ones, of allowing what is inside of you to come forth. Those creative energies, those impulses you are feeling to be *more* are there because you *are* more. It is time to come out of the closet, so to speak, because some of you have been hiding from your power. That's alright, its part of the human condition. There is no need to beat yourself up over anything that has occurred in the past at all, but rather to move forward and to know with certainty dear ones, that you are Divine creatures.

That spark of the Divine inside you is meant to create good things in this life. You are here to serve God and serve humanity in some way, because God serves you. It is not a one-way street here. You must accept all the ways that God does serve you. Open your heart to receive the love, the energy, the healing that is there for you. But also, *the way* - that is there for you as well. Of course you have free will choice, dear ones, and you are charting your own course, making your plans, making progress and moving forward, and so on, but also, any time that you are wondering "Where is my road map?" you can always take time to meditate with the Creator. Come into oneness with God, in whatever form or embodiment you relate to, and ask to be shown the road map - what is the blueprint that was laid before you *as your option*. We say that advisedly because it is *your option* - you have the option to do it or not.

The road map is not your command, but rather your desire. We feel, dear ones, that the road map is truly what you want in your heart, it is the plan that is in harmony with God, in harmony with why you are here. As you connect with that road map and you connect with what is Divine, right and perfect inside of you, of course you are going to be standing in your power, because you become that which you are creating your-self to be.

We encourage you, dear ones, to create yourselves to be the wonderful miracle-workers that you are. If you were to see the blueprint, it could very well say "miracle worker" upon it. You have miracles inside of you that are yet to come forth. Sometimes the miracle is just in who you become. Be open to exceeding your own expectations. Be aware that there is so much more ahead for you. We know that there is always going to be that daily grind in your day-to-day business world and working world, dealing with the people in your life and so on, but what we speak of is not exclusive of that. Because as you come into your power, you come into the awareness of All That You Are, and certainly you are *more* in every encounter, every situation, in every mundane detail of your life, you *are* more.

USING YOUR POWER FOR
MENTAL AND EMOTIONAL CLARITY

Living in your power can help you feel more in control of your life, which we know feels good to you sometimes. By control, we mean to have a sense that you know where you are going, a sense of what you want in your life and a sense of the wonderful person that you are. At the same time, you honor the goodness and the greatness in all your brothers and sisters. It just feels good to live from that perspective, trusting in yourself, trusting in your talents and abilities, yet honoring your humanness, respecting your vulnerability. Because to be human is to have emotions, to have sensitivities and to have feelings.

We know that sometimes you think of power as being almost a mental process of having strength and clarity, yes, but it is also an emotional state of awareness, of feeling that self-love and self-confidence, that sense of who you are and feeling good about yourself. It is when you have that heart-centered feeling emotion, that you can then move into the mental realms, and clarity is easier to achieve. Indeed, dear ones, anytime you are experiencing mental confusion, we encourage you to just take the time to move your energy from your head, down into your heart. Begin to feel the experience, feel the situation, feel the options, and then in your gut you will know whether or not it feels in harmony with God's plan or wish for you.

When we say "God's plan for you" that also includes you, because you have the essence of the Divine inside you. So when we speak of talking to God or a deity to get the blueprint, that is not something that is separate from you, but is an extension of you, another higher, grander, bigger aspect of you, the All That You Are.

MERGING WITH THE POWER OF THE HIGHER SELF

Work with your higher self, dear ones, it's the bigger you. Take some time in meditation to imagine yourself to be 10 to 12 feet tall, with an aura 10 to 12 feet wide, and that version of you is an all-empowered being of light. This *is* your higher self, the God Self, the bigger you. Integrate that aspect of who you are into your body. It may be easier at first to visualize it outside of yourself, but then bring it in. Then feel yourself in that big light body and feel yourself looking out from that perspective. That level of integration is what empowers you and builds your sense of self.

Even if there is a lot going on in your life, take some time to sit quietly and just be one with God. Truly, dear ones, with all your power, you have the ability to connect with God on such a strong and profound level. No matter what is going on in your life, keep your heart open. This is so important because your true spirit, the love and the beauty of All That You Are, emanates from your heart. Your heart center is the God center within you. God is pure, unconditional love, and to know that energy inside yourself and to share that energy with each other is so important. That will keep you on track with your power, always.

Keep anchoring the energies of your power, all the way down to your feet, throughout all of your body, but most importantly, keep your heart center open to the love of God, always, dear ones, and let that be your guide. This will keep the ego in check, keep your power heart centered, and keep it coming from a place of love. Then you will always do good, dear ones, you will always be acting on behalf of God and serving the greater good of all. Truly.

YOUR CREATIVE SPIRIT BRINGS POWER AND PASSION

Indeed, with all that is going on, we are wanting you to keep aware as well that your creative spirits are so alive right now. We spoke of the energies of passion, because this is a time to be passionate about what is important to you. It is a time to allow all those creative juices to be flowing in your life in remarkable and profound ways. This is not a time of holding back, dear ones. It is a time of truly moving forward with excitement in your life, moving forward with joyful anticipation of what you can create, staying open to the infinite potentials that are available to you.

So dear ones, let it fly, yes, let those creative spirits soar. Indeed we are wanting you to find your joy, find your bliss, to find what you can be passionate about and follow through with that with all your heart. Indeed, dear ones, we know that many of you are in a capacity to serve, to give, to help others. Be passionate about how much you can give and the quality of what you give. Honor that quality, honor your special uniquenesses, your gifts, your talents. This is the time that those talents are not meant to be put on the shelf, but are meant to come down off the shelf, yes? If you are wanting to be the artist, then put on the artist garb and *be* the artist. If you are wanting to be musician, then take the musician's clothes out of the closet and adorn yourself as the musician. If you are the magician, wear your cloak. Whatever your cloak, put it on and be the one you have always dreamed to be. Because the real truth is you are already that. It's already who you are. It's just that the time of wearing the masks is over, it's simply gone. Any of the masks that you used to wear, just don't fit anymore. It's not who you are. It is time to let the beauty, the real you, shine forth for all to see. And you are beautiful, dear ones, you are so precious. It is a time as well to feel that you are not alone in these endeavors. It is a time to rely upon your spirit, your higher self, your angels, your spirit guides, and, of course, the Christ, and all the Ascended Masters. They will always support you in your work and will always be there to give you that nudge, that positive encouragement, that guidance as to the direction that your heart is calling forth. Listen to your hearts, dear ones, and know that your heart speaks the truth to you. Your heart has all the answers.

Indeed, dear ones, it is not a time of second guessing yourselves either. It is a time of trusting yourself, trusting your instincts, and trusting that you are ready to move forward in your life. This may still be a time of laying the groundwork, laying the foundation and setting forth the plan, and that's alright, but put your passion into it. Put your heart and soul into it and let your creations truly be as beautiful as your spirit. That is the essence of our message for you tonight. We love you so much. Farewell for now, we are ONE."

CHAPTER 14

THE SHIFT IN THE COLLECTIVE CONSCIOUSNESS OF HUMANITY

A MEDITATION TO HEAL HUMANITY

Get as comfortable as you can, stretch your body a bit, and then relax completely. Gently come to be aware of a still, quiet centeredness inside you. Relax as we begin our meditative journey to serve the greater good of all man/womankind. Let us begin by inviting in the energies of God/Goddess/All That Is, and visualize white light as it streams forth from the heart of God. This light is the essence of pure unconditional love. Breathe in that white light, allowing it to touch every cell of your body, raising your own vibration to a heightened state of awareness.

Welcome in your own angels and spirit guides to come and join with you in this meditation, as they lend their energies of love and support.

Allow your own spirit to ascend into the higher realms. Become your higher self, free from the limitations of the physical realm. Perhaps you feel wings upon your back, or simply your own light body. Become aware of your freedom, your ability to move through the realms of consciousness to a higher place.

Begin now to visualize a beautiful gridwork of light that surrounds our Mother Earth at this time. Imagine now that we are joined in the higher realms by hundreds, even thousands of light beings, master teachers, healers, and embodiments of the energies of God/Goddess/All That Is. Take a moment now to feel yourself as part of this healing network of light beings, surrounding the Earth with a loving, healing energy.

As thousands, perhaps even millions of light workers and light beings from all over the globe join with us, we focus the energies of love and peace to radiate from the highest realms, through us, down to the core of Mother Earth.

Envision the gridwork in your mind's eye, the gridwork of light. Feel yourself a part of this gridwork of light, as we focus the energies of love and peace into the hearts of all of man/womankind and into the collective consciousness of humanity.

Accept and understand your power. Just like the "Hundredth Monkey" effect, collectively, with thousands or millions of light workers, you now shift the consciousness of humanity to a perspective of love and peace.

Allow the energies of change and transformation to move through the gridwork, through your own body, mind and spirit, and through the collective consciousness of humanity. Allow the energies of change and transformation in God's highest light to be known and felt throughout the world, in its highest and most positive expression.

As you continue to change the programming of the collective consciousness of humanity, allow the visions to come forth of a beautiful future that lies ahead, the best manifestations that can come. Allow the visions, the hopes, of the best that can be, to integrate into the gridwork, into the collective human consciousness. Our dreams, our wishes, our greatest hopes for humanity. See those things happening.

As we envision a healed and transformed humanity, envision the essence of God, or the essence of Christ or any God Embodiment to come into the hearts and souls of each living being on this Earth. Visualize each one of humanity to be a walking Christ, a walking God, holding the highest light and love. Send those energies throughout the gridwork, throughout the consciousness.

Take a moment to envision your own highest and greatest destinies. Open your heart and mind to be shown how it is that you are meant to serve the greater good, how you are meant to serve God and humanity. Take a moment to open to those visions, those understandings and those messages.

Take these last few moments to feel the loving presence of your guides and angels, and receive whatever healing energies or messages that you are needing at this time, keeping your heart open to receive all that you need.

Bring as much love into your heart as you can bear, feeling how loved you are, how special and precious you are.

As we bring our meditation into completion, take some deep breaths, and allow the energies of gratitude to be felt for all the light beings that are supporting you and all the planet right now. Allow the giving and receiving of thanks, knowing that you can return to the energy gridwork at any time you choose. There will always be beings of light there holding the energy, holding the love. Allow your higher self to gently find its way back to your physical body, taking some deep breaths to anchor the spirit to the physical, allowing the energy to come all the way down to your toes. Feel good about who you are. Allow the energy of contentment, completion and fulfillment. A job well done, dear ones.

MESSAGE FROM ONE CHANNELED
ON SEPTEMBER 21, 2001

ONE: "Greetings Dear Ones. Indeed it is a great pleasure for us to be with you fully in this way. We have enjoyed the meditation with you very much. We know that these are such challenging times, such difficult times indeed, but we are wanting to thank each one of you dear ones, for your good work tonight, for your prayers, your meditations have been so powerful and so incredibly helpful. You have each accessed the higher realms with more and more ease. Tonight, dear ones, you were truly united with the collective consciousness of humanity. Truly, your positive thought forms have made a positive impact. This is a time to not underestimate your power dear ones, it is a time to know that you can and do make a difference. This is the time that all the light workers have been preparing for. This is such a momentous time in your planet's history. It is a time truly, where the tides have turned. Where the awareness of the anger that has been building in the collective unconsciousness has been painfully made aware to all who have lived in peace.

It is not the end of peaceful times, dear ones, it is but the beginning of the transformation of the collective consciousness of humanity. We focused on that so much in our meditation tonight for good reason, because it was the collective of humanity that was brought under attack, not just New Yorkers or D.C.'ers, but it was the collective of humanity, to all peace-loving people of this Earth. But they shall not win, dear ones, you must know that in your heart. The energies of God and love will prevail. The number of peace-loving humans far, far outweigh the number of those who choose to dwell in hatred and fear.

You must stand strong in your love; stand strong in what you know to be right. And you know what is right in your hearts; you know that this massive wrong-doing that has occurred is beyond the present scope of understanding. The ramifications and ripple effect will continue for years, decades, perhaps even centuries, to come. But we want you to know dear ones, that that is not a bad thing. It is the memories of the pain that spur humanity to make change, to create less tolerance for those who perpetuate hate. It was not the angelic realm's wishes, it was not in God's heart, to create such suffering. It was the will of men, that brought the suffering upon this planet, this humanity. But these acts of hate created ramifications that will bring positive changes. We reiterate that because it is important that you not despair, that you not fall into fear that this now a downward spiral of pain. No dear ones, it is not, it cannot be. The will of humanity, the heart of humanity is too strong for that.

You see it now, rallied around the American flag. That is but a symbol of the pride of who you are, the pride of the freedom you have created. Its all right to rally together in that forum, but remember it is but one aspect of who you are. And then go to your churches or spiritual gatherings, and rally in the forum of oneness with God. Then come into your circles of friends and rally in what you can do as light workers, and come into all of your groups, your families, wherever they are and rally the energies of love and togetherness. And just how transformative that will be to this planet, IS the ripple effect that we speak of.

The transformations, the miracles, the power, the energies are just beginning to be known and understood. The power is beyond what you have imagined it to be. You must keep this perspective alive and strong because that is what quenches the flame of hate. It is the power of love. Understand that the power of love far outweighs the power that this judged evil may have. We say "judged" advisedly because the acts were an expression of rage, an expression of the pain that they have welled up inside of them. Think of those people that created this pain, what pain was inside of them? The collective consciousness of humanity must heal that pain. Seek not to fight it with more pain, but combat it with love and healing.

We know there are those who seek revenge in painful ways "eye for an eye" and we hope that those people in power come to more compassionate understandings at some point. You can send them love and energy for transformation and healing, so that they can come into more of love, more of compassion, so that no more innocent lives are lost. But dear ones know that even as you watch some of this "eye for an eye" this instant justice play out, there still needs to be the collective consciousness umbrella of love to support these processes so they are minimized, so conflicts are minimized and that healing and peaceful resolutions come about quickly. That is your goal as a collective through this process and we are simply verbalizing that which is already in your heart, in your higher selves, that which you know to be true.

We want you to know how powerful you are. Don't ever give up, dear ones. Don't give up on your dreams, your visions, your hopes for your future. There are some souls who are sacrificing their physical lives for this greater good. The beautiful human beings that were lost in these tragedies have collectively joined their souls together to say "This will not be in vain." Their souls live on. They have joined in the collective consciousness of humanity to lend their energies of support, to create positive change. It will happen, dear ones. The hatred of a few will not quench the love of the many. You must know that in your hearts.

Also know, dear ones, that many of you are meant to be the support-givers to those who find themselves lost in the pain and sadness. Speak your truth dear ones, and be that listening heart. Be the one that is giving of love, compassion and understanding to those who are in pain. Minister to the sick, to the ones who are sad, to the ones who are lost. Remember, if you are clear in your sense of direction as to where you are going and what you need to do to create your ultimate manifestation of your highest and greatest destinies, you uplift all who know you, all who are touched by your life. You help them to see the ultimate highest greatest destiny that they are meant to experience.

We wish to speak just for a moment of those precious souls that were on the plane that crashed in Pennsylvania. We only wish to bring them up briefly to let you know that there truly were heroes on that flight that saved the Capitol. That, we feel, was the target. We want you to know that those brave souls served as an example of the power of what some individuals can do. *That*, was part of the plan. Because those few, those handful of men who were so brave in that horrible moment of facing their own deaths, transcended their own human life, to something so great. Let those lives be an inspiration to those of you who are still gifted with your physical life to go about your day-to-day, to be the heroes, to be the ones who make a difference. You can do that dear ones, you have the power. It doesn't have to be on the scale of saving the world, but it is. Even if it is one person that you turn their heart around from a place of grief and sadness, or anger and hatred, into a perspective of love. That is happening all over this globe. And to those of us on the other side who can see it energetically, it is a beautiful thing.

We come in with so much energy and excitement tonight because we are excited about the transformations that are occurring now. These are no ordinary times. These are profound times. Be careful of your view, and the energy that you shroud it in. After these tragedies, you all needed to go through your grieving, your pain, feeling the collective sadness of humanity, yes, but it was necessary to understand the power of your humanity. Humans have such a profound depth of emotion that you experience your realities. The key is to remember that you do not need to stay stuck in any one emotion. Think of e-motion as energy in motion. So whether you feel the depths of pain or the heights of ecstasy, revel in that broad range of energy and emotion and understand that your power as humans is that you can choose where in that scale you wish to live, every day. Every day you can make that choice. That is God's greatest gift to you, the free will to know you can be whatever you wish to be. You can be the hermit, you can be the extrovert, you can be the hurting child, you can be the joyful dancer. You can be whatever is in your heart to be. You are not victims. It is important that you keep the energy of victimization tiny, very very tiny, like a pea that you can flick away. Think about that one, yes.

We see the energies of New York City, in particular, that were hit so hard. Visualize a bubble of white light around Manhattan right now. Just keep a big bubble of light all around that area. Send healing energy to all its peoples, to its landmarks, to all its buildings, to its very stones, to the trees, the plants, and to the glass. We say the glass because there is a lot of glass in Manhattan and glass is crystalline in nature, and has the ability to absorb energy. Send healing energy to all the crystalline structures of Manhattan. We felt that important to mention, because by supporting that energy structure, it speeds the healing of all involved.

The souls that have crossed over, please know that they are at peace already. They have been shown the grand plan. They are being shown the good that will come from their passings. It is sad that there had to be such high numbers to catch the attention of the world, but make no mistake about it, there is not a being on this planet that does not know it, and feel it, and understand the significance of it.

We also wish to mention the energies of our beloved friend, the Princess Diana. It was but four years ago that the world felt the crushing blow of her loss. And the energy that was created then, in the collective mourning of humanity, set up a vibrational resonance that now the collective consciousness of humanity finds again. And it is that familiar sense of pain and loss. With that comes a resolve. With that the energies are not stagnant, it comes in moving waves, moving forces of energy that then begin to take on their own process of moving, transitioning, and changing, and then moving forward. Understand that there is a process occurring that is greater than you can know. It's alright. We know you want to know it all now, but it's alright. You will know as time moves on. Be at peace with that. Know what you know now and be alright with that. Trust in your heart that good will come. The love of God will prevail.

Please know that you are not alone in these times. Reach out to your spirit guides, angels, and of course, the Christ - you must know that Christ is involved in every step of this healing process for humanity- the blessed Mother Mary, as well as the Moon Goddess, who watches over this Earth with her protection of love. Her energies are consistent, as are your

Mother Earth's energies. She will always love and nurture you. Allow yourself to be nestled in the bosom of Mother Earth. Take time to be at one with nature, because your own soul programming will find comfort in walking upon Mother Earth, feeling the leaves, rolling around in the grass, looking up at the beautiful sky, seeing the moon. These are programmed into the human soul to bring a sense of comfort. Indulge yourself in those comforts, because that too brings about healing of the collective consciousness of all of humanity, the collective soul.

Begin to see yourselves as one soul family of Earth. The Earth Family. Hold that image in the energy gridwork surrounding the planet, of one family of Earth. We like that. Feel Mother Earth embracing all of humanity, and the Father Sun basking the Earth in his warmth and love. Hold those images of light, of hope for the future, and you can and will make a difference. Make no mistake about it dear ones, these are powerful times of transformations.

That is the essence of our message for your tonight. We love you with all our hearts and souls and we speak on behalf of all your spirit guides and angels. We send you our heartfelt love and healing energy for tonight and through all time. We are One. Truly, dear ones, we are one. Let that be your chant, your mantra, not just our sign-off. We are here with you always. Good night, dear ones. We are ONE."

"It is important for each one
to make a personal choice to either be
centered in fear or in love. This is the
most powerful choice you can make –
to think love, feel love, radiate love,
teach love and BE love.
The soul's choice is always love,
and to every question, the answer is
always love."
~ ONE

CHAPTER 15

COMMUNICATING WITH YOUR LOVED ONES ON THE OTHER SIDE... A CHANNELER'S PERSPECTIVE

I have been very blessed to be aware of my ability to communicate with the "other side" for about 16 years now. I have primarily focused on channeling angels and spirit guides of the higher realms. This work has been incredibly rewarding and now I can't imagine life without channeling my guides and angels for myself and others.

I'd like to share with you some of my experiences in communicating with the other side, and some techniques to help you make those connections yourself. I also hope to bring the old concepts of the Séance into a new millennium perspective.

About 9 years ago I had an amazing channeling session with a client of mine, whose husband had committed suicide a few years before. The spirit of her deceased husband appeared to me during the session, and said he wanted to ask for her forgiveness. He realized in the afterlife how much emotional pain he had caused her and he wanted me to express to her how sorry he felt. I relayed the messages and it was so powerful that I could feel his emotions expressing through me. The second she verbalized that she forgave him, a huge beam of light came down from above (it felt like God!) and his soul was completely enveloped in this brilliant light. I clearly saw his spirit rise up into the Light with an incredible radiant joyfulness. He ascended right before me! I was so awestruck that I wept profusely, along with my client. It truly felt as though I had facilitated and witnessed a genuine miracle.

That experience made me realize how powerfully healing it can be to work with the other side. To help someone connect with a loved one who has died builds a bridge of understanding and healing that is beyond words.

I am grateful to John Edward, a famous Medium from Long Island, New York, who has a wonderful television show called "Crossing Over." It is still amazing to me that our society has opened up enough that major television networks, like CBS and the Sci Fi Channel, would broadcast to millions of people every day, a genuine medium in his prime, communicating with those who have crossed over. I love the commercial for the show: "The afterlife will be televised!" These are exciting times indeed! He provides validations by bringing through information about the family that he would have no way of knowing. His courage, to be under such high public scrutiny, and do what he does so well, is remarkable and deeply appreciated by those of us in this field. I personally want to thank him for awakening so many to the truth of our souls.

I have been bringing through these kinds of validations in my channeling sessions for years, but I purposefully avoided calling myself a medium. It has taken me years to be more comfortable about using the "m" word. To call myself a medium felt like an invitation to be challenged. I feared attracting new clients that would demand specific private details, and who would be quick to deem me a fake for failing to pass their tests. Who needs that kind of stress?! I still don't want to attract those kinds of clients, but I'm no longer afraid of them.

Over the years, more and more of my clients were asking my guides to relay messages from their loved ones on the other side. It seemed that every time I would channel for my meditation groups, someone would ask for a message from a deceased relative. Often others would jump on the bandwagon and instead of the group enjoying compelling questions and answers that would benefit everyone, messages from loved ones began to dominate my open channeling circles. Although I appreciated the importance of those personal messages, I really wanted to keep the dead people out of my meditation groups! So, I decided to set aside specific evenings devoted to talking to deceased loved ones. My spirit guides and my clients were thrilled. Thus, I started having séances in my home, or as I prefer to call it, "An Evening with your Loved Ones on the Other Side."

SÉANCES

A Séance... for some that word conjures up an image of a cold, dark room, a large round table, and a spooky-looking medium who starts flailing her arms around as the spirits move her. As she trances out and her eyes roll to the back of her head, a booming voice, not her own, commands the room. The participants, called "sitters," are awe-struck as the eerie rapping sounds send shivers down their spines. Then, suddenly, the lights flicker and the table levitates off the floor! The medium then, hopefully, speaks messages from the great beyond. Oh, the drama of the olden days!

I like to think that I've updated my Séances for the twenty-first century. I welcome ten people into my warm living room, and invite them to get comfortable. The scent of freshly baked cinnamon coffee cake blends nicely with my nag champa incense. I have plants, angels, candles and crystals tucked in every corner of the room. As people come in they are invited to light a candle in memory of a loved one.

A few years ago when my best friend, Vicki, died of cancer at the age of 48, I made a candle garden for her memorial service. It is set on a beautiful crystal cake plate with a large pillar candle in the center, with many votives and silk flowers all around it. I held onto this candle garden for years, never wanting to disassemble it. In preparing for my first séance, I heard Vicki's spirit suggest that I use her candle garden to allow people to light a candle in memory of a loved one. It lends a bit of sacred ceremony to the occasion.

With the living room sofa and chairs loosely set up in a circle, I begin the evening by leading a 15-minute guided meditation to help everyone open up to loving energies. We welcome in the energies of God/Goddess, Christ, Mother Mary, the Archangels, the Ascended Masters, and all of our own guardian angels and spirit guides. We then invite the spirits of our deceased loved ones to join with us. This gives everyone the opportunity to begin feeling the presence of the spirits themselves and come into a peaceful state of being. I keep the light of God strong around our circle so that only loving beings on the other side can participate. I feel safe in this work as I know there is nothing "evil" that can hurt me or anyone in the room.

A MEDITATION TO CONNECT WITH YOUR LOVED ONES

To do this on your own, find a quiet place to sit and relax. Visualize white light from the heart of God pouring into your heart and soul. Allow yourself to surrender to this beautiful healing light. Just let go and trust that you are safe in God's pure Divine light. Stay in this light until you become aware of your own light body, your soul or higher self.

Once in that higher state of awareness, gently invite a loved one on the other side to come and be with you. Allow yourself a moment as you begin the process by remembering how the energy of that person felt when you were with them. Start the process by imagining that they are with you. The reality of it is that they *are* with you when you call in their spirit, but you have to open the door by first believing that it is true.

As you begin to feel the spirit of your loved one, allow your emotions to flow - if that is part of your healing process. Try to hold the focus that the energy of your loved one is still with you. Allow yourself to say, telepathically or verbally, whatever you want to say to them. Then take a deep breath and relax again. Keep the focus on their presence, and allow some quiet time just to be with their energy. In those moments, keep your heart open to receiving love from them. This time also allows them the opportunity to telepathically communicate messages to you.

Do this as often as you need, but remember that your loved one wants you to heal and get beyond your grief. Often a loved one on the other side can become a best friend or spirit guide that is with you purely for love, support and even fun. Open your heart to the many blessings and gifts of spirit that your loved ones on the other side have for you.

IDENTIFYING DIFFERENT ENERGIES OF SPIRIT

In my experience I have found that there are can be a whole range of energies that you can experience on the other side. When developing your communication skills with other realms, it is important to be aware of what types of energies you can run across or call forth. It is always a good idea to begin your communication work by calling forth an aspect of God's energy to strengthen your own aura of love and affirm a feeling of protection.

To give you a sense of the energy spectrum you can experience, think about how light and beautiful the energy of the Christ or Mother Mary would feel. In contrast, now think about the most difficult person you have had to deal with in this lifetime, and how *their* energy feels to you. Their energy or aura might feel dense, like there is anger or some other heavy emotional energy in or around them. This contrast loosely symbolizes opposite ends of the spirit energy spectrum. When someone dies, depending on who they are and what happened to them, their energies could feel anywhere in this spectrum and even beyond.

Before you call forth the spirit of a loved one on the other side, consider the state of their soul. Chances are, if your loved one was a happy and peaceful person while living, connecting with them on the other side would feel the same way. However, if your loved one died with a great deal of anger or distress, you may tap into some uncomfortable energy especially if you try to contact them too soon after they have died. In these situations, send their soul love and healing prayers to assist them in their transition.

When I was asked to contact a young woman who had committed suicide just a couple months prior, her soul was not talkative at all, and really did not want to be disturbed. I clearly saw her, but she was completely wrapped in a cocoon of healing energy. I relayed that she was still in her healing process and that perhaps we could try to connect with her at a later time. In the meantime, I was clearly guided that we were to send her prayers of healing energy to support her. I knew that she would not be stuck there forever, and that in time her soul would heal.

I believe our soul goes through a healing process upon the death transition that is intended to clear and transform those kinds of difficult energies. Our angels, spirit guides, and loved ones who passed before us, work with our soul to create peace and deeper understandings of our lifetime on a soul level. This is a process of integrating the lessons that were meant to be learned in this lifetime. Since we transition in death to a non-linear existence, it is difficult to put a time frame on this healing process. For some it could be instantaneous with death, or it may seem to take days, months or years.

Be aware that many factors may influence the feelings you potentially could experience when you connect with someone on the other side, such as how recent their death was, the way in which the person died (peaceful or violent, anticipated or sudden) and their soul evolution level. Some souls incarnate here to learn some pretty heavy lessons, and some souls are purely angelic beings that incarnate as humans to serve a higher purpose. If you have any question about the state of being of your loved one, send healing prayers first. Whenever it feels comfortable to you, start the telepathic communication by sending them love. Then open your heart to feel their love for you.

It was only three days after my best friend Vicki died, that she came to me in spirit and showed me that she was fully integrated into the bliss of God. She and I had channeled the Christ Consciousness together in the early 1990's, so she was very familiar with the higher realms. Even though her life review process may have taken more than three days in our linear perspective, I was greatly comforted by knowing she had found her home in the higher realms and was with Christ.

MY PROCESS OF OPENING TO SPIRIT

As I studied more about traditional séances, I learned that it is not unusual for the medium to use a spirit guide to help with the process of bringing through messages. Since I started out this work as a channeler, it was a natural progression to use my spirit guides for mediumship. As I described earlier, I create my channeling state of consciousness by focusing on my breath and visualizing white light pouring into me from the heart of God. Usually within a minute or so, I begin to feel a heightened sense of awareness. In that state, I welcome ONE to come and blend with me. This is always a beautiful and loving experience for me.

For many years, I have developed a deep and trusting relationship with ONE because they have consistently proven themselves to be in harmony with the energies of God and Christ. I'm honored to say that they have never disappointed me and have always amazed me. I can easily surrender to their loving energies, because I have total and complete trust in them.

As ONE blends with me, I allow them to speak directly through me. When I am in this altered state of consciousness, I am aware of everything ONE says. I can "see" with my mind's eye, and "hear" telepathic communications from spirit very clearly. The people I channel for hear the words, but I'm watching the movie! It is truly a multi-sensory experience.

MESSAGES FROM THE OTHER SIDE

I always explain up front that there are never any guarantees in this work. I have found that if someone has pre-set ideas of particular information that must come through to prove that this is real, that the spirits may not cooperate. We have to understand that in this process, *they* choose what message comes through, not you, and not me. We should honor and respect them enough to be grateful for whatever message or validation they choose to convey.

Some spirits are very talkative and have a lot to say, often with details and specifics about their life to prove and validate their presence for their loved ones. Sometimes the spirits come through in a loving and blissful state simply wanting their loved one to know they are at peace and their love for them has survived.

While there are no guarantees that spirit will say what you want them to say, I always let my clients know that I take this work very seriously and I promise that I will do the very best I can to serve them well. I believe they can feel my sincerity. I also express my respect for the depth of pain that grieving a loved one can create. Death of a loved one is probably the worst emotional experience we as humans endure. The profound depth of love and caring we can feel for another soul is equal in energy to the depth of pain and suffering we can feel in grief.

As we begin the séance, ONE "looks" around the room and telepathically asks for a spirit to offer their name and a message to their loved one who is present in our circle (the "sitters"). Often I will see a face rush up to me, from a specific direction, and hear a name. Sometimes they will say their name or the name of the person they are appearing for. ONE and I then relay those messages. In one séance a strong female spirit flew at me from straight across the room and said clearly her name was Kathryn and she was here for her granddaughter. As we spoke that, the woman sitting directly across from me gasped and said her grandmother's name was Kathryn. Kathryn then began to relay a powerful message for her granddaughter in the bold style she was known for in life. Typically, the energy and personalities of the people come in quite clear.

In another séance, a woman's deceased husband came in and was really working his charms on the women in the room. He said he wished he could give every one of them a kiss. Suddenly we were interrupted by another spirit named Paul, who felt this guy was getting too much attention. The woman gasped as Paul was her <u>second</u> deceased husband! Everyone who knew Paul was laughing hysterically as it was totally Paul's personality to step in and demand equal time! Séances can really be a lot of fun sometimes.

Often questions are asked of the sitters to get clarification on what is coming through. It's as though when a positive response comes from the sitter, it strengthens the connection and more information can then flow through. The recognition seems to bring them closer. However, if I'm getting a clear presence of a spirit named Mildred and no one in the room is acknowledging that they know who Mildred is, then we have to send Mildred away. In that case, the spirit might feel disappointed that she was not able to bring through her message. I often wonder whether these are wandering spirits who actually don't "belong" to anyone in the room or whether one of the sitters just plain forgot about poor old, dead Aunt Mildred.

TRANSLATION TECHNIQUES

The professional mediums I have seen in action (John Edward, Suzane Northrop and John Holland) have developed systems of communication in symbols that help support the process of bringing through specific details. These mediums are among America's finest and you can rest assured they are genuine.

For example, as John Edward often explains on his show, a spirit may be indicating another individual as above, below or beside them. This has universally been interpreted as parent, grandparents, aunts, uncles, are above; siblings, spouses, friends and colleagues appear to the side; and children appear below. These can be viewed as generational hierarchy symbols. I use this system as well, but I recently had a spirit come in with a sisterly (beside) energy and it turned out to be the woman's mother. As the information continued to come through, it was shown to me that this mother felt more like a sister to her daughter than a mother, and that the two had been sisters in a past life together.

There are many other symbols that may come through, but the spirits have to work within each medium's frame of reference or basis of knowledge. As the medium "sees" and "hears" things, the best we can do is relay it verbatim and work with the clients in its proper application and interpretation.

Spirits will relay their messages via visual, auditory or sensory tactics. Mediums must learn to trust what comes through because self-doubt and second-guessing can create our greatest blocks. Trust and confidence are the benchmarks of a good medium.

PHYSICAL BRAIN VS. SOUL MIND

I have come to understand a distinction between our physical brain and our soul mind. Think about this for a minute, you die; your brain is dead, gone. What's left? Thankfully, your soul! Your soul has a mind, a consciousness, an awareness of itself, where it has been and what it has experienced. However, the "soul mind" certainly can have selective memory. The soul remembers what was important to it on a <u>soul level</u>. Once passed on, Uncle Charlie may not remember where he left the key to the safe! However, he will likely remember who he loved, the lessons he learned in his life, his favorite things, friends, or places. For example I recently contacted a young man on the other side, who kept saying "baseball, baseball, baseball!" I concluded that this boy must have loved baseball. The woman cried as she shared that he loved baseball so much that they buried him with his bat! The soul remembers what is important to it.

Interestingly, sometimes a person's perspectives or opinions may change after their death transition. It is as though the blinders come off and the soul has a more expanded awareness. They can now step back from their limited ego-self or personality, and see the bigger picture of life. This "higher self" perspective can result in the releasing of prejudices or judgments that the person may have made during his life. For example, I once channeled for a gay man, whose father had died. His dad, in physical life, was completely unaccepting of his son's lifestyle choice. When I connected with his soul on the other side, the father was now giving his blessings to his son and his partner. The father was truly happy that his son had found someone special to share his life with, and the prejudice was gone. Unfortunately, the client rejected the message stating that his father "never would have said that." Although his father had found acceptance, the man chose to hold on to the anger he still felt for his father. As much as I tried to build that bridge of understanding between them, I believe the mutual healing may have to wait until this man's transition, when his Dad greets him with on the other side with unconditional love.

FINAL THOUGHTS

If you miss your loved ones on the other side, be open to creating a new relationship with them. Consider their souls to be alive and well, just living in another dimension. Leave them at rest if you feel that they would want that, but don't be afraid to reach out to them in love. They will let you know in their own way and in their own time, that they are okay. They may appear to you in a dream, and that can be a genuine visitation, or you may just suddenly think of them out of the blue. That could be them, whispering in your ear, or knocking their picture off the wall. Spirit can communicate with us in so many different ways. Keep your heart open, and they will find a way in.

The information they may communicate is rarely earth-shattering. However, if it is a genuine connection, I believe the messages will be loving and will ring a bell of truth. When I channel messages from the other side, I know I'm not making up this stuff. I simply deliver messages and pray that my work always maintains the highest level of integrity. I look forward to my work ahead as my medium skills continue to sharpen. As I said, the key to strengthening my abilities as a medium is to trust what comes through without second-guessing myself. I hear my guides laughing as they tell me "Let's 'super size' that medium please!"

I feel so blessed to have such wonderful guides on the other side. Honestly, I think everyone has wonderful spirit guides and angels. You should take the time to get to know just how wonderful they truly are. It is a joy and a privilege for me to commit my life to serving God by serving humanity as a channeler of the angelic realm. The mediumship aspect is a delightful bonus that allows me to help people heal from grief and come to a place of peaceful completion with their loved ones. I want to show people how to develop this new relationship with their loved ones in spirit.

I believe the ones we love the most, those who are closest to us, are there for us in spirit after they pass over, and can be a spirit guide for you on the other side. Do not worry that you might be holding them back from anything by talking to them telepathically and keeping your heart open to giving and receiving love energy with them. They don't want to hold you back either. They don't want you to stay in grief too long. They want to gently encourage you to feel love in your life and create joy, again and again.

I've had some lively spirits come in, wagging a pointed finger at their living loved one, saying "Don't take crap from anyone!" And some gently encourage us to follow our dreams. Just imagine what your loved one would be saying to you now

- you know what they would say. If it is loving and supportive, I'm sure you are right. Take that into your heart and feel their love. I send you my love as well, and I wish for you the peace that God's love brings.

Chapter 16

Messages of Hope
for an Awakened Humanity

A Message from the Arcturians

"Energies from extraterrestrial forms are coming through Terra at this time, and we welcome this opportunity to greet you. We are the Arcturians and we come in great love for all of you. We thank you for inviting us. We wish you to know that many of your extraterrestrial friends feel deep love and profound connection with this branch of humanity, because we are connected to you ancestrally through our DNA. The extraterrestrials that come to support this planet will come in physical form in the future. However, we presently choose to deal on other dimensional levels because third dimension can create stress upon our light bodies that are difficult at times.

Fear not, because there are many beings supporting humanity in a way that wishes for the highest and best of humanity to come into transformation. Those of us who see the greatness within humanity are very strongly believing in your abilities to transcend the present difficulties to experience a life on Earth that you presently can only dream of. We have seen the visions clearly through the multiple various future time lines that can occur for humanity and we wish to deliver our message of hope that each one of you can lend your positive contributions to these utopian visualizations for this planet because it <u>can</u> occur, it can be here for you, on this Earth. We have hope that it can be manifested within your present time lines.

We want you to feel the peace that can be. We want you to learn from the civilizations that have destroyed themselves in previous planetary existences because you do <u>not</u> have to destroy yourselves. There is much hope for what can be. It is out greatest hope that you can hold that hope strong and clear and bright in your hearts and project that clear bright projection out into the universe to help it come into manifestation. We want you to know that there is much love for you on many dimensional levels and we want very much for you not to fear, but to keep your hearts open to the infinite love that we know is yours inside your hearts. We will surrender our energies now and allow the Energies of ONE to come back into this body. Greetings and farewell." [Arcturians complete]

A MESSAGE FROM ONE

"Greetings, dear ones! We are the Energies of ONE and it is a great pleasure for us to share our love and our insights with you. We have been asked to speak on the energies of 2003 and beyond, and we are delighted to progress your timeline forward to share with you our perspectives of your possible futures, as well as share our guidance for an awakened humanity.

Humankind has some powerful and important choices to make this year. While there are many so-called "war mongers" in your government who are focused on perpetuating fear, there are also growing numbers of peace keepers. It is important for each one to make a personal choice to either be centered in fear or in love. This is the most powerful choice you can make – to think love, feel love, radiate love, teach love and BE love. The soul's choice is always love, and to every question, the answer is always love.

There is an underlying sense of urgency to maximize your life here – physically, mentally, emotionally and spiritually, as though your spirit is encouraging you to get your affairs in order and get this lifetime right. This inner compelling, will move many people towards making needed changes in their lives. A mediocre life becomes unacceptable and the strong desire to manifest the inner needs becomes undeniable. The main focus will be in creating more harmony and enriching the quality of every aspect of your life.

We encourage you, dear ones, during these times, to take the time that you need for your own mental, emotional, spiritual and physical well-being. Take the time to go within. Ask your body, ask your spirit, ask your emotions, ask your mind – what do I need right now? What do I need to do to heal, to grow, to evolve, and to move forward. As you take care of yourself, dear ones, remember that it is not selfish, because then you live a life that serves as an example for others. Teach by living the example of what it is to be self-actualized and integrated with the God-Self. Simply living your life in a way that honors all life, certainly honors your own. This teaches others to respect their own needs physically, mentally, emotionally, spiritually and also globally.

We feel that each one of you here, on a spiritual path, is a responsible Earth citizen. It is important to you to do what is right. Be respectful of the Earth and of your brothers and sisters in humanity. To help you in that endeavor, dear ones, we want to remind you to always be true to yourselves, honor your integrity, and honor the truth within. Move forward with that integrity and that truth. Truly, dear ones, the answers are within you.

EXPANDING YOUR LIFE'S PURPOSES

We feel that each one of you is on a very powerful path of teaching, healing and supporting others. We want you to not resist those roles as they present themselves to you, dear ones. Embrace the opportunities to serve those who need your help. We sense that there are many troubled souls out there these days...those who may feel lost or abandoned, or those who suffer through grief. There are also many who are living in fear. Of course, the antidote for fear is love. So stay centered in love, dear ones. Live with a love-centered state of being, a love-centered state of body, mind, spirit, soul, communication, and sharing. Staying centered in love teaches others how to be centered in love, and that is so needed right now.

We feel that each one of you here (and reading these words) is a light worker, one who is meant to shine the bright light for those who may be lost in the darkness... darkness, perhaps, of their own illusions, and the darkness of their own fears. There are many, many souls lost in that darkness. And so be that shining light, dear ones, we know it, we see it in you. We know that you are here, truly, to make a positive difference to help people in very deep and profound ways. Embrace those roles as teachers and healers, because you are so needed right now. We hope that you can honor just how precious you are. If you ever need reminding of that, dear ones, call in your angels and spirit guides. We are always happy to shower you with love and adoration. We truly do adore you, and we do honor and respect you for your courage, the courage to be here now, by choice, to help humanity through these very transitional times.

We want you to be more aware of your power, your strength and your ability to feel unconditional love and compassion for your brothers and sisters in humanity. We know that you are peace keepers and that being a peace keeper truly is part of your life's purpose. Your mission here is to foster peace, to create peace and share peace with others. That is done by embodying pure love and compassion, and developing a clear sense of oneness with God/Goddess/All-That-Is. It is in that oneness that you acknowledge that you are more than just a body. That opens you to experience a sense of connection with all of humanity and with Mother Earth as well. As you extend your energies you can even feel oneness with all the Universe.

The Peace Keepers' Force

After the profound tragedies of 9-11-01 many have sought understanding of the higher purposes that must arise from such pain. This was certainly an event of intense magnitude that was profoundly felt energetically in the hearts of millions of souls. This particular event was chosen to stand as a key turning point in the shift of consciousness of humanity to a greater awareness of how pain and suffering in the collective consciousness needed to be healed.

As we have shared before, those who ascended into light that day vowed that their lives would not be lost in vain, and have united in their efforts for the cause of peace. We call these souls the Peace Keepers Force and many have added to their numbers since that time. Many thousands of light beings and transcended souls have also joined the cause and much work is being done in the higher realms to support the global healing process.

The integration of the lessons learned is an important part of the healing process. This is not to dwell on the pain of the past, but rather to choose to recognize that there is pain in the consciousness of humanity that needs to be healed and is ready to be transformed. By focusing on the healing process and staying centered in compassion, you can uplift the whole consciousness of humanity to a place of allowing peace and love. This simple prayer: 'May humanity allow peace' speaks to the power of surrendering to what is already there, inside each human soul.

We also wish to tell you, dear ones, that there is every reason to hold onto your strongest hopes and visions of what humanity can become and your vision of global peace. Also envision love spreading throughout the planet, along with the energy of Creation itself, which allows creative resolutions to the conflicts to come about. The essence of creativity will help evolve humanity. Include those visions in your prayers as well.

The Return of Joy

We wish to say, dear ones, that in the wake of 9-11-01 and the pain that came about, you could almost feel guilty to go out and create too much fun. Just as when you lose a loved one, there's a natural grieving and mourning time that you would feel that having fun doesn't quite seem right, and somehow disrespectful to the mourning process. Be very aware that your loved ones on the other side would want you to speed through your grieving and healing process as quickly as possible. They would want you to come into acceptance, peace, healing, honoring and respect. They would want you to understand the greater reasons or purposes served by their life and death. They would want you to heal and come through that process, and most importantly, they would want you to feel joy again. And so, for more than a year now, all of humanity has mourned, you have grieved appropriately. There is now understanding, there is now respect, and there is now wisdom. The Peace Keepers are committed to working hard to evolve humanity, and to prevent those things from happening again. Let that bring you peace, and honor their memory by allowing the return of joy into your life.

Also know, dear ones, that in your day-to-day experiences, there are people that love you. It is very important to keep the energies of giving and receiving love in balance. Be very aware of the love that is in your life and take the time to fill yourself with the energy of gratitude for those who love you, because that completes the cycle of giving and receiving. Balanced energies of giving and receiving love allow you to give even more love. Stay in that loop, dear ones, and remember that the same concept applies to your abundance in life. As you give of yourself abundantly, keep yourself open to receiving abundantly as well. You are worthy, dear ones, because the quality of that which you have to give is so precious, valuable and needed. Place a very high value on all that you have to give and then give it with all your heart and soul. Create with joy for Creation's sake, do God's work, for God's sake, and do humanity's work for humanity's sake.

Keep that flow moving and going in your life in every way that you can apply it – relationships, work, career, fun, and yes, give fun, humor, laughter and joy to others. Then stay open to receiving fun, laughter, joy and play from others. If you find yourself lost in the seriousness and the heaviness of each day, you're missing a big beautiful, joyful, exciting part of your life that is wanting to burst forth. That is the inner joy that needs to be expressed within each one of you.

In that process, dear ones, you can't forget the importance of the joy and the beauty, and the richness that you can experience in this physical body on this beautiful planet. Feel the richness that you have here, the deliciousness that you have here, the beauty of your mountains, streams, flowers, and all the fruits of your world. Enjoy those pleasures with the fullness of all that you are, with a hearty sense of gratitude and joy. Just be aware of how that one enhancement can transcend every area of your life and uplift your whole life to a whole new level of pleasure, enrichment and fun. You deserve it dear ones, it is here for you.

We see so many that are that banquet and are afraid to eat, and who starve to death standing in front of the banquet. Not you, of course, but you know who they are. So eat hearty at the banquet of life, yes, stuff yourself with as much joy, pleasure, beauty, creativity and fun as you possibly can, because others need to be shown how to take that in for themselves. So once again, living your life in a delicious, exuberant, joyful, wonderful and fulfilling way shows the way for others. Do not underestimate the importance of that gift. Be the way-showers. Be the ones that have the most fun, alright? Because that teaches so much. We hope that you can take that into your hearts and apply it in a way that is joyful, exciting and meaningful for you.

We also wish to remind you: Create! Create! Create! Allow yourself the freedom to express yourself creatively in some way:

make music, paint, write, draw, sing, dance and doodle! Yes, be creative, dear ones, as a source of infinite pleasure for the soul and for the God-Self as well.

DEEPENING YOUR RELATIONSHIPS

The quality of your relationships will definitely be a major focus this year. In the quest for a deeper and richer experience of life, it will become very clear to you when a relationship is disharmonious to your soul. The underlying fear thoughts that life here on Earth is short and precious will compel people to make changes in their relationships. In the past, unfulfilling marriages have often dragged on, each clinging to the love they once felt for each other. In these powerful times, the awareness of disharmony can no longer be denied, and people will choose to move on. That's not to say there won't be some strong and solid relationships. In fact, the quest to find one's soulmate has never been hotter. There is a strong sense of the quality of love that one seeks to experience, and those who do find a soulmate will work harder at keeping a clear sense of harmony in the union.

Same sex marriages will be on the rise, as more people begin to recognize the androgynous nature of their soul. There will be more acceptance and understanding that soul love is not always gender exclusive. Despite opposition to this trend by religious groups, many more states will expand the definition of 'family' to include same sex unions. Many who choose this lifestyle are great teachers of love and tolerance. In time, humanity will heal its prejudices, and grow to honor choices that are motivated by love.

The key to deepening all your relationships is to focus on honoring the God within each of you. Look deeply into each other's eyes and really look into their soul. Allow the energy of love to radiate from your eyes like healing beams of light. This healing gaze is a powerful gift you give each other. Give it freely and do not underestimate the healing power of your soul!

We hope our messages have been helpful to you in preparing yourself for these very expansive energies. May you go forth and live your life in a way that is honoring of the joy and the beauty inside your spirit! We send you love and blessings through all time. We are ONE."

TRUTH GIVES YOU FREEDOM FROM ILLUSION

When you speak your truths, you are adding such an important and very positively needed vibration to the earth right now. These are times in which it becomes excruciatingly difficult for people to remain in illusion. You may even know some people that are very much caught up in a false belief system. We see some people that have blinders on in some areas of their life. Even the one whose body we are using, this one that you know as Terra, once upon a time had those blinders on. Many years ago, when her first marriage was struggling, she would say to herself and others "I am happily married... I am happily married... I am happily married..." even when that did not resonate with her inner truth. She would say this mantra because it helped her to hold onto that illusion. We also feel that in these types of situations where you have convinced yourself of a happier reality (that may not mirror what you are genuinely feeling inside yourself), then you could create complete chaos in your life to bring the truth to the surface. In our beloved Terra's case, when she had to keep convincing herself that she was happy, circumstances practically had to blow up in her face to bring it to her awareness that change was needed. Once she could admit her own inner truth, she had the strength to achieve her freedom.

We are simply wanting to help you to short-circuit that process. You see, you don't have to have things blowing up in your face for you to understand the reality of what you are truly feeling in your heart and soul. We are simply bringing into your awareness the importance of being completely and sometimes brutally honest with yourself. When you can know and speak the truth to yourself, you are empowered to make positive changes in your life.

These are times in which those illusions, those false masks, cannot work for you any longer. The truth that rears up inside of you can no longer be denied. This may apply to your life in some small way or in perhaps some big ways. That is for you to discover for yourselves.

Stay Centered in Compassion

More importantly, even if you are now content with your life and your energies, you may be seeing and observing how this inner battle between illusion and truth is affecting people that you know and love. Therefore, this message may be to help give you clarity and understanding of what some of your brothers and sisters of humanity are going through right now. Many of you are the teachers, the light bringers, the way showers, the counselors, and the healers. You are the ones that are meant to help the ones who are lost in their illusions. So when you see these types of experiences that your brothers and sisters in humanity are creating for themselves, we wish for you to be loving and compassionate with them. Understand that letting go of an illusion about themselves is sometimes the hardest thing to let go of. It is when one's soul can come into more awareness of the truth, that the true nature of their spirit begins to shine. Their true feelings emerge and their greatest potentials open up. This is when someone gets more into their power and steps more into the God Self, more into the awareness of the All-That-They-Are. That is a beautiful process, dear ones.

Just be compassionate, patient and understanding with yourselves and others. Do not judge yourself or others, but rather keep your heart open. Know that in your beautiful humanness, there will always be those ups and downs of emotions, those complexities that bless your life from time to time. Embrace those delightful complexities as opportunities. As our beloved friend Mary says "This has come to Bless me." Yes, that truly is such a powerful approach to life that we commend her on that one. It is truly inspiring.

Golden Nuggets of Empowerment

Open to the perspective of taking a step back to observe each situation in such a way that you can begin to understand there is a gift underneath all of this. That even in pain and chaos, there is a precious nugget of gold hidden inside for you, to pull out of it. The golden nuggets of self awareness and of expansion are priceless treasures indeed. And so dear ones, we wish you to go on a treasure hunt! We wish for you to rummage through your life and find those golden nuggets of lessons and "Ah ha!" moments that you can grab hold of and say "Yes! This is why I have come through this. This has made me stronger. This is the lesson I gained, that I can now teach and share with the world!"

Equally so, there is a treasure hunt for all of your beautiful and magical qualities, your incredible gifts of spirit, your profound abilities to teach, to heal, and to help inspire others. Dear ones, gather these golden nuggets into your heart, into your solar plexus and fill yourself up with all these golden nuggets of truth, your golden nuggets of genuineness. That is what we wish for you, dear ones. Fill yourself with so much gold that your whole body radiates a golden beautiful light. The true self will shine, when you acknowledge that it is already there. We speak of the golden nuggets metaphorically to help you in your process of building that golden light within and to help you be more aware of your process of empowerment and enlightenment. But know, dear ones, that the real secret is that you already radiate pure Divine golden light. This true self is just waiting for that perfect moment to reveal itself, and to shine forth for all the world to see.

The other secret is that you can just flip that switch any time you like! You can choose to radiate God's light and love and be the All-That-You-Are in any moment that you choose to acknowledge your true self. This is what they call being 'self-actualized.' This is what they call 'enlightenment.' This is what they call 'living in your integrity.' That is our wish for you, dear ones, to know with every fiber of your soul and being what it is to live in your pure golden integrity. That is truly who you are.

We are happy to share with you our visions of who we know you to be, to help you to open to that awareness, to that knowingness within your heart and soul that no one can ever take away from you. There will be many who cannot see your light, but that does not mean that you cannot see it for yourself. Own it, dear ones. Know who you are. Move forward in your life with that assumption, that you *do* radiate golden light from the heart of God. Be All-That-You-Are! That is our message for you, dear ones. We hope you can take that into your hearts and nourish it. Our deepest love and blessings to you, through all time and space. We are One."

CHAPTER 18

LOVING GUIDANCE AFFIRMATIONS FOR MEDITATION AND PERSONAL GROWTH

In preparation for one of my recent meditation groups, ONE channeled through me the following set of positive affirmations. I typed them onto little cards and each person was able to draw one randomly from a beautiful cloth bag that was hand-made for me by a dear friend. As each person drew a card and read it, we were all amazed at how the chosen affirmation was such a perfect match to the person drawing it. We then went into meditation focusing on the issue that the card brought to light. I offer these to you, to select the ones that touch your issues, and use them in meditation or as positive affirmations for your personal growth and spiritual development. Enjoy!

I am guided to love myself more fully, body, mind and spirit. No judgments, only love.

I am guided to open my heart to loving others more, honoring the God within each one. In this process, I will always love myself and honor the God within me.

I am guided to honor my creativity. There is a light and beauty inside me that must shine forth. I honor the blessings that pour forth from allowing my creativity to be expressed.

I am guided to open to receive more. I am worthy to receive infinite love and prosperity, as I blend with the endless flow of God's great universe.

I am guided to honor my spirit and practice my spirituality in a way that brings me joy. I know there is infinite peace inside me and I open to the many blessings of my spirit.

I am guided to listen to my inner truth. There are no secrets or illusions that block my knowing. Because I have no fear, I am open to knowing everything there is to know about myself and my world. I am open to hearing the truth of who I am.

I am guided to release my old pattern of worrying. I know in my heart that there are no burdens that I need to carry. I surrender the challenges to God and trust that all is well in my life. I open to more blessings of joy.

I am guided to honor my life's purposes. I accept that there are no small purposes in my life. Everyone I touch and everything I do serves the higher good in some way. I am open to exploring more of who I am!

I am guided to honor my need for freedom! I am completely free to express all that I am. I am free to explore my world and seek joy! I am free from my mental and emotional burdens of the past. My spirit is free to know God.

I am guided to honor the powerful being that I am. There is no more hiding from my power because I accept that my power can hurt no one. I accept my power with grace. I know that I will always use my power for the loving good of all.

I am guided to open to receive more healing energy. I surrender the issues of the past and bask in the glory of healing light that pours from the heart of God. In this sacred space, I feel the light and beauty of my spirit.

I am guided to honor my need for fun. I accept the responsibilities of life with ease and open to the silly and humorous side of life. I laugh easily at myself and my world. I create fun for myself and others.

I am guided to feel passionate about my life. There is nothing mundane in who I am and why I am here. There is an excitement in the air and I feel alive with the infinite potential of all that I can create!

I am guided to release all patterns within me that were self-limiting in the past. I am now open to surrendering to the beautiful flow of life that my higher self, in oneness with God, creates for me.

I am guided to reflect on the fulfillment and satisfaction that I have created for myself in this life, up to this time. I open my heart to feel the gratitude and fulfillment for all that I have and all that I am.

I am guided to trust more. I surrender the inner questioning and allow God and my higher self to work their magic in my life. I trust the truth I know in my heart and I trust that God will always provide for me.

I am guided to honor my choices. There are no regrets. I accept all of my past and honor the blessings that have come into my life. I feel confident that I will always choose lovingly for myself.

I am guided to open my heart to God/Goddess. There is a message that God has for me today. I accept the Divine guidance that pours forth. I submerse myself in the well of infinite love that God endlessly provides.

I am guided to expand my awareness into the All That Is! I release the limitations of the past and accept that there is much more in the world for me to discover... about life, about myself, and about God.

I am guided to seek more balance in my life. I open to receive more love so that I can give more love. I surrender to my needs and allow myself to take good care of me. I love me enough to pay attention.

I am guided to allow the winds of change to blow easily in my life. I surrender any fear of change I may have had in the past to allow new and glorious creations to be birthed into my life. I am guided to allow my higher self to emerge fully into my physical manifestation. I no longer feel separate from my higher self as I accept the God that I AM!

* * * * *

A few years ago, ONE and I co-created a different set of positive affirmations. I channeled most of them, but a couple of them were modified from various books I was reading at the time. I give my thanks to Paul Ferrini[5], Sanaya Roman and Duane Packer[6] and Carole Daxter[7], for your inspiring words which helped me to personalize some of these affirmations.

I am in my *Right Livelihood* because *I Love what I do* and the universe *rewards me abundantly* for my gifts. *I am paid extremely well* for all that I do.

I thank God/Goddess, with a grateful heart, for all that I am, all that I have, all that I will have and all that I will become. So be it!

I have an endless supply of energy to do all the things I need to do. As I nourish my body with love, it serves me very well.

I have all the time I need to get everything done that I need to do. I have a clear knowing of my priorities and time is my friend.

I choose to bring more *joy and laughter* into my life *every day* and I take delight in sharing that joy with everyone.

I trust in myself enough to know that I will always be in the right place at the right time, doing the right thing. I trust in Divine synchronicity.

I honor the *God/Goddess* within me and I honor the *Divine purposes* that I have come here to fulfill.

I am a perfect creation of God. I see and acknowledge the beauty of my body, the brilliance of my mind, the warmth of my emotions and the light of my spirit.

I now feel *total freedom* to express the pure and joyful spirit of my soul. *I am happy to be me!*

I see beyond all illusions of the past and it has made me **strong**. I look at my life with joy and *feel the Freedom* to **Now** live the life I have always dreamed of. It is Mine!

I now know with clarity that my future lies before me like a blank canvas on which I may paint the beautiful colors that are the masterpiece of my life.

I am worthy enough to: be adored, receive abundance speak with God, play with children and feel at home in the company of angels.

I successfully achieve all my goals *with remarkable ease* as infinite blessings of good fortune constantly appear in my life. *Because I deserve it!*

There is only love. No matter what goes on around me, I can always feel the deep core of love in my soul and create infinite peace. I know the bliss of God.

Bask in the Bliss of Oneness with All That Is. I am one with God, never separate, never alone never powerless. I proclaim my Divinity!

I trust the Divine Plan and choose to consciously co-create my life with God/Goddess. I proclaim my power and honor my sacred place in the heart of God.

I honor my Divine Gifts! I acknowledge the Healer that I am, the Teacher that I am, the Saint that I am, the Angel that I am, and the God that I am!

The Essence of Christ dwells within me. His love is my love. His healing power is my healing power. His feet on the Earth are my feet on the Earth.

My Angels are always with me. My Angels love me, protect me, encourage me and honor me. I accept their many gifts!

I choose to feel *Gratitude* for all the good in my life for the loving people, for my special gifts, for my continuing abundance and for the endless flow of love that comes to me.

Life presents me with infinite opportunities to *fulfill my dreams* and to create *MAGIC* as I willingly explore the unknown with *Positive Expectation*!

The Universe now provides me with an *infinite abundance* of love, money, and joyful relationships. My feelings of gratitude amplify my success even more.

* * * * *

I hope you will use these affirmations to remind you of who you are and what you are capable of creating. I encourage you to write down or type the ones that really touch your heart and post them in your home or office where you can see them, repeat them and integrate their truth into every fiber of your being.

Love & Blessings from Terra and ONE

Acknowledgments

I would like to take this opportunity to thank the people in my life who have blessed me with much love and support. I offer my heartfelt gratitude to my husband Jeff, my Mom Arlen, my Dad Jim, and my sisters, Shari and Betty for the powerful foundation of love and strength that each of you gives to me. To my wonderful in-laws, Jacky, Stan, Jason, Janet, Jackie, Dot and Jack, thank you for your love and for welcoming me into your family with open arms. I thank my amazing personal assistant Kiki, who is a God-sent blessing and a great joy in my life.

I thank my wonderful and loving friends whose love and encouragement keep me going... Mary, Janet, Meredith, Kate, Lorraine, Joyce, Doris, Joe, Lynne, Gloria, John, Jeannie, Jeanne, Kathe, Eileen, Peggy, Kathleen, Christie, Dan, Mya, Irene, June, Linda, Andrea, Rhianna, and all my wonderful meditation group friends and channeling clients. My heartfelt gratitude to my Mom for her important help in transcribing my tapes and for her constant love and support. My love and thanks to my "brother" Bill for opening the door to my channeling ability. I'd also like to thank my business consultant, Bob Staskel for his valuable insights. My heartfelt thanks to Len X Filipowski for creating the beautiful music on my meditation CD. I also send my love to Vicki, my friend on the other side, who's spirit still blesses me. My love and deepest gratitude to all of you.

I also give my heartfelt thanks to God, Christ, Mother Mary, Sai Baba, the Archangels, ONE, and all my wonderful angels and spirit guides, for the infinite blessings of my life. I pray that their light always guide me and keep me centered in love. May my service to God honor the sacred gifts bestowed upon me.

BIBLIOGRAPHY

[1] *Past Lives Future Loves* by Dick Sutphen, Pocket Books (paperback 1984 ISBN: 0671543636)

[2] *Messages from Michael* by Chelsea Quinn Yarbro, published by Berkley Publishing Group, 390 Murray Hill Parkway, Dept. B, East Rutherford, NJ 07073 (ASIN: 0425104370)

[3] *Discipleship in the New Age*, Vol. 2, p. 179 by Alice A. Bailey, Lucis Press, 120 Wall St., 24th Floor, New York, NY 10005.

[4] *How to Teach Ascension Classes* By Joshua David Stone published by Light Technology Publishing, available through Melchizedek Synthesis Light Academy, www.drjoshuadavidstone.com.

[5] *The Way of Peace* by Paul Ferrini, published by Heartways Press, P.O. Box 99, Greenfield, MA 01302

[6] *Creating Money* by Sanaya Roman and Duane Packer, published by H.J. Kramer, Inc., Tiburon, CA

[7] *Pure Love* by Carole Daxter, published by H.J. Kramer, Inc., Tiburon, CA

The Book of Seance by Tom Cowan, published by Contemporary Books, Inc., Two Prudential Plaza, Chicago, IL 60601

I highly recommend these books and give my heart-felt thanks to the authors for their inspirations.

RESOURCES

For wonderful meditation crystals, channeling crystals, altar pieces, crystal singing bowls, and much more, check out my favorite metaphysical resource at www.starwomancrystals.com.

For information about becoming ordained in the Order of Mechizedek, check out www.worldlightfellowship.org or visit the World Light Center at www.worldlightcenter.com.

Here is a list of some of my favorite meditation music:

Name of Group/Artist	Name(s) of CDs
2002	Wings, Chrysalis, Land of Forever
Liquid Mind	Slow World, Unity, Balance, and Serenity
Patrick Bernhard	Atlantis Angelis
Deuter	Reiki:Hands of Light and Garden of the Gods
Dean Evanson	Healing Sanctuary and the Tao of Healing
Coyote Oldman	Tear of the Moon
Mike Rowland	And So to Dream, Fairy Ring
John Serrie	And the Stars go with you
HALO - Heavenly Angelic Light Orchestra	AngelicLight- Celestial Song

Deva Premal	Essence, Embrace and Love is Space
Aeoliah	Angels of Healing Vols.1- 4
Oracle	Oracle
Steven Halpern	All of his are great - Inner Peace, Gifts of the Angels, Spectrum Suite are some of my favorites
Merlin's Magic	Reiki Music and The Heart of Reiki
Terry Oldfield	Illumination
Valley of the Sun	The Eternal OM
Music by Marcey	Inward Harmony (1-800-843-3240)

SPIRITUAL COUNSELING
WITH TERRA SONORA

Rev. Terra Sonora is an Interfaith Minister with World Light Fellowship. She is available for private spiritual consultations, in person or by phone. She channels her loving spirit guide, "ONE", a celestial/angelic entity who is here to teach and heal with love.

In a private session, "ONE" can introduce you, by name, to your angels and spirit guides. They will assist you in every aspect of your spiritual growth and soul evolution. "ONE" can view the akashic records and provide information about relevant past life experiences and past life connections with people you love. The angels can often establish a communication link with deceased loved ones to bring through messages from the other side. The insight and guidance brought through "ONE" regarding relationships, health, life purpose and your spirituality are profound.

Terra is very proud to have established a solid, excellent reputation with hundreds of extremely satisfied channeling clients all over the world. She is available for both private spiritual counseling appointments and group work. Gift Certificates are also available.

You may contact Terra at:
Terra Sonora
P.O. Box 2251
Poughkeepsie, NY 12601
(888) 485-0111
www.angelchannel.com

Here are a few comments from some of Terra's clients:

"As always, thank you for another beautiful channeling session. But thank you more for teaching me and inspiring me to make my light shine brighter. I am forever grateful that our paths have crossed." Meredith Altimari, Pembroke, NH

"I played the tape from my session with 'ONE' over and over and woke up the next day with more peace than I can remember having in a long time. I am so grateful. I think in today's world you are truly needed!" Annie L., New Paltz, NY

"I want to say thank you to you and ONE for a most wonderful experience. It was without a doubt the highlight of my visit to America. I think it was the reason for going there — to meet you and ONE." Dr. Magdel S., South Africa

"As I spoke with ONE, I received so many confirmations of things that I've felt so unsure about. ONE patiently answered every question and concern I had. Our meeting was, without hesitation, the most incredible experience of my Life." Ginny Katona, Kingston, NY

NEW! FROM TERRA SONORA
PERSONALIZED GUIDED MEDITATION TAPES

Accelerate your personal and spiritual growth with an individually customized guided meditation tape channeled from the Angelic Realm! Terra Sonora will first spend some time discussing with you your personal needs and goals. She will then blend with the energies of Ascended Masters and Angels to create a personalized guided meditation tape to help you connect with the Divine within, clear any personal issues, heal yourself and/or empower you to manifest your dreams! If there is a particular Ascended Master, Archangel or aspect of God that you would like to deepen your relationship with, those attunements can be given in the meditation as well.

Your own personal angels and spirit guides will be invited to participate in the creation of a customized Guided Meditation Tape and will include a personal channeled message from ONE. The meditation may be set to music if you like, or created without music if you would prefer to play your own music in the background or work in silence. The guided meditations will generally be between 20 and 25 minutes long.

Personalized Meditation Tapes are $100 which includes the initial consultation, audio tape, tax and shipping. They are available on audio cassettes only and not on CD at this time. To order, send check or money order for $100 to Terra Sonora, P.O. Box 2251, Poughkeepsie, NY 12601 with your name and phone number. She will contact you to set a time to discuss your needs and goals. Gift Certificates also available.

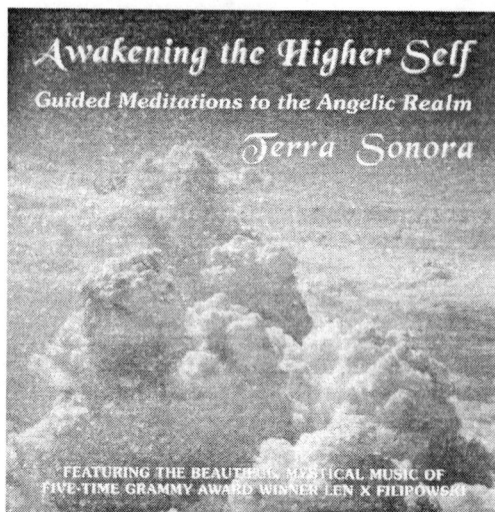